TEACHER GUIDE and ACTIVITY RESOURCES

Teacher Notes
- Math Centers
- Math Readers
- Practice Games

Activity Support Masters
- Math Centers Resources
- Gameboard Copymasters
- Workmats

HOUGHTON MIFFLIN HARCOURT
School Publishers

www.hmhschool.com

ISBN 10: 0-547-27819-5
ISBN 13: 978-0-547-27819-3

12 13 0982 18 17 16 15 14
4500466878

Contents

Grab-and-Go!™ Kit Overview

Teacher Notes: Math Centers

Teacher Notes: Games

Teacher Notes: Math Readers

Blackline Masters

Blackline Masters (continued)

Grab-and-Go!™ Kit Overview

The Grab-and-Go!™ Kit is a collection of literature, activities, and games that can be used in the math classroom. The Kit's ready-made components minimize preparation time for you and provide engaging and fun-filled ways for your students to review and reinforce valuable math skills.

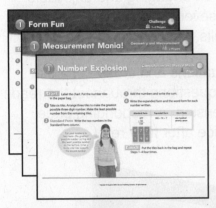

Kit Components

MATH CENTERS

These ready-made, easy-to-follow activities help you reinforce or extend mathematical concepts and skills.
There are three types of Math Centers – Computation and Mental Math, Geometry and Measurement, and Challenge.

LITERATURE

Integrate reading and math with these engaging stories. Through these readers, you can connect math topics and concepts to each other and to daily life.

GAMES

Practice skills and apply concepts with these ready-to-use interactive math adventures. Students can play these games in pairs or small groups.

TEACHER GUIDE AND ACTIVITY RESOURCES

This valuable resource provides everything you and your students need, including teacher notes for activities, literature, and games, and activity support masters.

Using the Grab-and-Go!™ Kit

The Grab-and-Go!™ Kit provides teachers with streamlined and enjoyable ways to help students review, reinforce, and extend math concepts and skills. The math center activities, games, and readers are designed for flexible usage – students can work independently, in pairs, small groups, or with guidance from the teacher.

- Games help students practice essential math skills in an engaging and enjoyable manner. Your students will want to play these games several times, allowing them ample hands-on practice and mastery of essential skills.

- Math Readers integrate math skills with real world situations and cross-curricular subject matter to engage student interest. Interactive questions throughout the readers focus on key concepts and support student comprehension. A responding page includes questions and an activity for additional practice after they read.

- Math Centers cover three themes: Computation and Mental Math, Geometry and Measurement, and Challenge. Colorful and creative visuals guide the student through the steps. The clear step-by-step format helps the student easily access, process, and reproduce the concepts and skills.

- Grab-and-Go!™ Teacher Guide and Activity Resources (See following page for more details.)

Using Grab-and-Go!™ Teacher Guide and Activity Resources

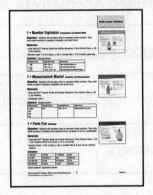

Teacher Notes for Math Centers include

- objectives for each activity
- materials needed for the activity
- answers to all the activity questions

Teacher Notes for Math Readers include

- key skills and concepts
- story summary
- essential vocabulary words
- responding answers

Teacher Notes for Games include

- objectives for each game
- materials for the game
- game instructions

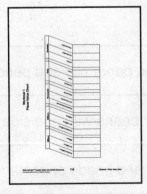

Activity Support Masters include

- Math Centers Resources
- Gameboards
- Game Resources
- Workmats

Suggested Alternatives for Math Manipulatives

Math Manipulatives	Suggested Alternatives
Balance Scales	clothes hanger, paper cups, and string
	bills made from construction paper and markers
	number cards, spinners
	real coins, buttons
	paper clips, string and beads, or pasta
	clock face with two lengths of string fastened to the center for hands
Factor Triangles	index cards with one factor in the center and two factors in each corner
	circles of colored construction paper that are cut into sections
Fraction Strips	index cards
Fraction Tiles	index cards
	cans, boxes, balls, cones, modeling clay shapes
	shapes cut out of different-colored construction paper or cardboard
	grid paper cutouts
	construction paper, paper clip and pencil
	coins, washers, or beans with one side painted
Unit Cubes	paper clips, string and beads or pasta

1 • Number Explosion Computation and Mental Math

Objective: Students will use place value to represent whole numbers. They write whole numbers in standard, expanded, and word forms.

Materials:

- *Grab-and-Go!™ Teacher Guide and Activity Resources*, Three-Column Chart, p. 38 (1 per student)
- Number Cards 1–9 (3 of each), p. 69, or number tiles 1–9 (3 of each), paper bag

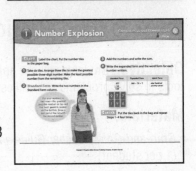

Answers: Sample answer:

Standard Form	Expanded Form	Word Form
986	900 + 80 + 6	Nine hundred eighty-six
+ 144	100 + 40 + 4	One hundred forty-four
1,130	1,000 + 100 + 30	One thousand, one hundred thirty

1 • Measurement Mania! Geometry and Measurement

Objective: Students will use place value to represent whole numbers. They write whole numbers in standard, expanded, and word forms.

Materials:

- *Grab-and-Go!™ Teacher Guide and Activity Resources*, Four-Column Chart, p. 39 (1 per student)
- Centimeter rulers

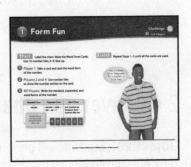

Answers: Sample answer:

Measurement	Standard Form	Expanded Form	Word Form
Length:	845	800 + 40 + 5	Eight hundred forty-five
300			
300			
245			

1 • Form Fun Challenge

Objective: Students will use place value to represent whole numbers. They write whole numbers in standard and expanded forms, focusing on zero as a placeholder.

Materials:

- *Grab-and-Go!™ Teacher Guide and Activity Resources*, Three-Column Chart, p. 38 (1 per student); Word Form Cards, p. 42 (1 per group)
- Number Cards 1–9 (3 of each), p. 69, or number tiles 0–9 (one set per student), scissors

Answers:

1,263,409	503,246	17,483,206	2,048
702,369	403,568,157	603	2,695,704
312,465,708	50,468	62,704,319	6,123
987,456,301	315,210	37,015	207,369

Check students' expanded versions.

2 • Size It Up Metric! Computation and Mental Math

Objective: Students will use appropriate units for measurement. They will use tools to solve problems and will estimate and measure objects in metric units.

Materials:

• *Grab-and-Go!™ Teacher Guide and Activity Resources*, Three-Column Chart, p. 38 (1 per student)
• Centimeter ruler

Answers: Sample answers: tissue box (height); 12 cm; hand length; 13 cm. Sample order: tissue box: 13 cm; notepad: 14 cm; pencil: 18 cm; computer screen: 24 cm; math book: 30 cm.

2 • Measurement MATHO Geometry and Measurement

Objective: Students will select and use appropriate units for measuring. They will choose an appropriate metric unit of measure for finding the length, mass, or capacity of an object.

Materials:

• *Grab-and-Go!™ Teacher Guide and Activity Resources*, MathO Cards, p. 43; Object List, p. 44 (1 per student); Object Cards, pp. 45–46 (1 per group)
• Scissors, 25 counters or cubes

Answers: 1. g; 2. m; 3. cm; 4. km; 5. m; 6. mL; 7. L; 8. kg; 9. mL; 10. cm; 11. g; 12. g; 13. dm; 14. m; 15. mL; 16. m; 17. m; 18. m; 19. L; 20. cm; 21. kg; 22. m; 23. g; 24. m; 25. mg; 26. mm; 27. mL; 28. mg; 29. mm; 30. dm; 31. g; 32. m; 33. dm; 34. g; 35. g; 36. m; 37. mL; 38. m; 39. dm; 40. km.

2 • Conversion Challenge Challenge

Objective: Students will perform conversions within a measurement system. They will convert among metric units of length.

Materials:

• *Grab-and-Go!™ Teacher Guide and Activity Resources*, Five-Column Chart, p. 40 (1 per student); Circle/Spinner, p. 47 (1 per group)
• Transparent spinner, Number Cube Patterns, p. 107, or 4 number cubes

Answers: Sample answer: 24 dm = 2,400 mm.

3 • What's My Factor? Computation and Mental Math

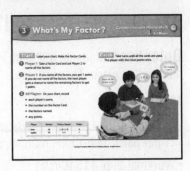

Objective: Students will find all the factors of whole numbers written on factor cards.

Materials:

• *Grab-and-Go!™ Teacher Guide and Activity Resources*, Four-Column Chart, p. 39; Factor Cards, p. 48 (1 per student)

Answers: Sample answers: 20: 1, 2, 4, 5, 10, 20; 32: 1, 2, 4, 8, 16, 32.

3 • Prime Figure Geometry and Measurement

Objective: Students will identify prime and composite numbers. They will identify a figure by the number of its sides. Then they will identify that number as prime or composite.

Materials:

• *Grab-and-Go!™ Teacher Guide and Activity Resources*, Three-Column Chart, p. 38 (1 per student); Figure Cards, p. 49 (1 per pair)

Answers: Card 1: 4, composite, 1, 2, 4; Card 2: 8, composite, 1, 2, 4, 8; Card 3: 48, composite, 1, 2, 3, 4, 6, 8, 12, 16, 24, 48; Card 4: 17, prime, 1, 17; Card 5: 16, composite, 1, 2, 4, 8, 16; Card 6: 3, prime, 1, 3; Card 7: 8, composite, 1, 2, 4, 8; Card 8: 8, composite, 1, 2, 4, 8; Card 9: 5, prime, 1, 5; Card 10: 10, composite, 1, 2, 5, 10; Card 11: 6, composite, 1, 2, 3, 6; Card 12: 32, composite, 1, 2, 4, 8, 16, 32; Card 13: 11, prime, 1, 11; Card 14: 64, composite, 1, 2, 4, 8, 16, 32, 64; Card 15: 10, composite, 1, 2, 5, 10; Card 16: 5, prime, 1, 5; Card 17: 12, composite, 1, 2, 3, 4, 6, 12; Card 18: 6, composite, 1, 2, 3, 6; Card 19: 6, composite, 1, 2, 3, 6; Card 20: 24, composite, 1, 2, 3, 4, 6, 8, 12, 24.

3 • Prime-O MATHO Challenge

Objective: Students will find the prime factorization of a number. They will play a game and find all the prime factors of two- and three-digit numbers.

Materials:

• *Grab-and-Go!™ Teacher Guide and Activity Resources*, Two-Column Chart, p. 37; MATHO Cards, p. 43 (1 per student); Factor Cards, p. 48 (1 per pair)

• Two-sided counters for each pair

Answers: 42: 2, 3, 7; 18: 2, 3, 3; 60: 2, 2, 3, 5; 20: 2, 2, 5; 33: 3, 11; 16: 2, 2, 2, 2; 66: 2, 3, 11; 75: 3, 5, 5; 63: 3, 3, 7; 45: 3, 3, 5.

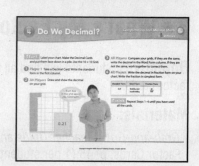

4 • Do We Decimal? Computation and Mental Math

Objective: Students will read, write, and order decimals through the hundredths place. They will use a 10 × 10 grid to represent decimals.

Materials:

- *Grab-and-Go!™ Teacher Guide and Activity Resources*, Decimal Cards, p. 50 (1 per pair); Two-Column Chart, p. 37 (1 per student); Centimeter Grid, p.59
- Workmat 2, p. 115 (Circle)

Answers: Sample answers: three tenths: 0.3; one tenth: 0.1; seventy-one hundredths: 0.71; fifteen hundredths: 0.15; thirty hundredths: 0.30; eight hundredths: 0.08; seven tenths: 0.7; thirty-four hundredths: 0.34; forty-three hundredths: 0.43; three hundredths: 0.03; ninety-six hundredths: 0.96; six tenths: 0.6.

4 • One Form to Another Geometry and Measurement

Objective: Students will read and write decimals and relate decimals to fractions that name tenths, hundredths, and thousandths. They will change money values into standard decimal, word, and fraction forms.

Materials:

- *Grab-and-Go!™ Teacher Guide and Activity Resources*, Three-Column Chart, p. 38 (1 per student); Money Cards, pp. 51–52 (1 per student)

Answers: 2, two, $\frac{2}{1}$; 0.05, five hundredths, $\frac{1}{20}$; 1.75, one and seventy-five hundredths, $1\frac{3}{4}$; 0.05, five hundredths, $\frac{1}{20}$; 7.20, seven and twenty hundredths, $7\frac{1}{5}$; 0.10, ten hundredths, $\frac{1}{10}$; 0.25, twenty-five hundredths, $\frac{1}{4}$; 1, one, $\frac{1}{1}$; 0.50, fifty hundredths, $\frac{1}{2}$; 0.75, seventy-five hundredths, $\frac{3}{4}$; 1, one, $\frac{1}{1}$; 0.60, sixty hundredths; $\frac{3}{5}$; 0.60, sixty hundredths, $\frac{3}{5}$; 0.65, sixty-five hundredths, $\frac{13}{20}$; 0.91, ninety-one hundredths, $\frac{91}{100}$; 0.50, fifty hundredths, $\frac{1}{2}$.

4 • Fraction to Decimal Bingo Challenge

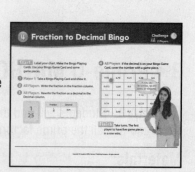

Objective: Students will relate decimals to fractions that name tenths, hundredths, and thousandths. They will change fractions to decimals and record the equivalent fractions and decimals on a chart.

Materials:

- *Grab-and-Go!™ Teacher Guide and Activity Resources*, Two-Column Chart, p. 37 (1 per student); Bingo Playing Cards, p. 53 (1 per pair); Bingo Game Card, p. 54 (1 per student)
- 40 counters or cubes

Answers: $\frac{1}{4}$, 0.25; $\frac{1}{25}$, 0.04; $\frac{4}{5}$, 0.8; $\frac{2}{25}$, 0.08; $\frac{3}{25}$, $\frac{3}{25}$, 0.12; $\frac{1}{1}$, 1; $\frac{5}{8}$, 0.625; $\frac{4}{25}$, 0.16; $\frac{1}{2}$, 0.5; $\frac{2}{5}$, 0.4; $\frac{12}{25}$, 0.48; $\frac{7}{8}$, 0.875; $\frac{1}{5}$, 0.2; $\frac{16}{25}$, 0.64; $\frac{3}{4}$, 0.75; $\frac{3}{8}$, 0.375; $\frac{1}{8}$, 0.125; $\frac{7}{25}$, 0.28; $\frac{7}{10}$, 0.7; $\frac{3}{10}$, 0.3; $\frac{1}{10}$, 0.1; $\frac{3}{5}$, 0.6; $\frac{9}{10}$, 0.9; $\frac{21}{25}$, 0.84.

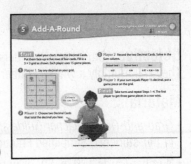

5 • Add-A-Round Computation and Mental Math

Objective: Students will use addition and subtraction to solve problems involving decimals.

Materials:

- *Grab-and-Go!™ Teacher Guide and Activity Resources*, Three-Column Chart, p. 38 (1 per student); 3 × 3 Grid, p. 55 (1 per student); Decimal Cards, p. 50 (1 per pair)
- 20 counters or cubes (10 of each color)

Answers: Sample answer: Card 1: 0.67, Card 2: 0.35, Sum: 1.02; Card 1: 0.15, Card 2: 0.37, Sum: 0.52.

5 • Get Around! Geometry and Measurement

Objective: Students will use addition to solve problems involving whole numbers and decimals. They will measure classroom objects and record the measurements, rounding to the nearest tenth.

Materials:

- *Grab-and-Go!™ Teacher Guide and Activity Resources*, Three-Column Chart, p. 38 (1 per student)
- Paper, a book, a box, a pennant, floor tile, centimeter ruler, and a meterstick

Answers: Sample answer: floor tile = 10.2 cm + 10.2 cm + 10.2 cm + 10.2 cm; Perimeter = 40.8 cm.

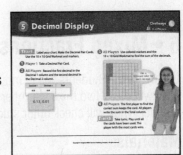

5 • Decimal Display Challenge

Objective: Students will use addition and subtraction to solve problems involving decimals. They will use centimeter grid worksheets and place-value charts to model adding and subtracting decimals.

Materials:

- *Grab-and-Go!™ Teacher Guide and Activity Resources*, Three-Column Chart, p. 38 (1 per student); Decimal Pair Cards, p. 56 (1 per group) Centimeter Grid, p. 59
- Workmat 1, p. 114 (Place-Value Chart), Workmat 2, p. 115 (Circle), colored markers

Answers: 0.07 + 0.7 = 0.77; 0.67 + 0.2 = 0.87; 0.9 + 0.06 = 0.96; 0.25 + 0.25 = 0.50; 0.35 + 0.53 = 0.88; 0.4 + 0.44 = 0.84; 0.8 + 0.9 = 0.17; 0.08 + 0.09 = 0.17; 8.23 + 51.6 = 59.83; 0.13 + 0.01 = 0.14; 42.36 + 5.7 = 48.06; 27.4 + 0.86 = 28.26; 7.23 + 4.08 = 11.31; 22.54 + 18.93 = 41.47; 74.82 + 6.1 = 80.92.

6 • Fraction Fix Up Computation and Mental Math

Objective: Students will understand the concept of multiplication of fractions. They will multiply a whole number and a fraction.

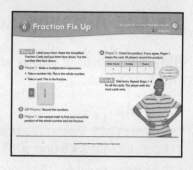

Materials:

• *Grab-and-Go!™ Teacher Guide and Activity Resources*, Three-Column Chart, p. 38 (1 per student); Simplified Fraction Cards, p. 57 (1 per pair)

• Number Cards 1–9, p. 69, or number tiles 1–9, scissors

Answers: Sample answer: $9 \times \frac{1}{3} = 3$.

6 • Fruitful Fractions Geometry and Measurement

Objective: Students will multiply a whole number and a fraction to find recipe measurements.

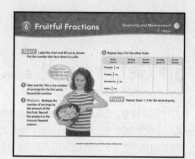

Materials:

• *Grab-and-Go!™ Teacher Guide and Activity Resources*, Five-Column Chart, p. 40, (1 per student)

• Number Cards 1–9, p. 69, or number tiles 1–9, scissors

Answers: Sample answers:

Sevings	$\frac{1}{2}$ cup pineapple	$\frac{3}{4}$ cup oranges	$\frac{1}{6}$ cup strawberries	$\frac{2}{5}$ cup apples
1	$\frac{1}{2}$	$\frac{3}{4}$	$\frac{1}{6}$	$\frac{2}{5}$
2	1	$\frac{3}{2}$, or $1\frac{1}{2}$	$\frac{1}{3}$	$\frac{4}{5}$
3	$\frac{3}{2}$, or $1\frac{1}{2}$	$\frac{9}{4}$, or $2\frac{1}{4}$	$\frac{1}{2}$	$\frac{6}{5}$, or $1\frac{1}{5}$
4	2	3	$\frac{2}{3}$	$\frac{8}{5}$, or $1\frac{3}{5}$

6 • Mixed Fractions Challenge

Objective: Students will compute and perform simple multiplication of fractions. They will make two mixed numbers using number cards and multiply to find the product. They will check other students' answers.

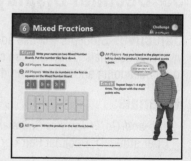

Materials:

• *Grab-and-Go!™ Teacher Guide and Activity Resources*, Mixed Fraction Boards, p. 58, (2 per student)

• Number Cards 1–9, p. 69, or number tiles 1–9

Answers: Sample answer: $5\frac{2}{3} \times 6\frac{1}{4} = 35\frac{5}{12}$

7 • Data Spin Computation and Mental Math

Objective: Students will record the results of spinning a spinner in a chart. Then students will make a bar graph of the data.

Materials:

• *Grab-and-Go!™ Teacher Guide and Activity Resources*, Circle/Spinner, p. 47; Three-Column Chart, p. 38; Centimeter Grid, p. 59 (1 per student)

Answers: Check students' charts and graphs.

7 • Geo-World Geometry and Measurement

Objective: Students will graph a given set of data using a bar graph. They will identify two-dimensional figures in their environment. They will display their findings in graph form and interpret the graph.

Materials:

• *Grab-and-Go!™ Teacher Guide and Activity Resources,* Three-Column Chart, p. 38; Centimeter Grid, p. 59 (1 per student)

• Five different-color crayons or color pencils

Answers: Make sure students' graphs match the data they collected in the 3-column chart. Make sure their interpretation and summary of the data are correct.

7 • Is This Seat Taken? Challenge

Objective: Students will use tables and graphs to interpret data. They will practice finding the mean, median, mode, and range of data.

Materials:

• *Grab-and-Go!™ Teacher Guide and Activity Resources,* Two-Column Chart, p. 37 (1 per student); Data Deck Cards, p. 60 (1 per group); Satellite Gameboard, pp. 61–62 (1 per group)

Answers: 1. Blue is the favorite color; 2. 20; 3. 15; 4. 4; 5. mean = 16.5, median = 18.5, mode = 20; 6. 10; 7. 9; 8. 7; 9. mean = 78, median = 79, no mode; 10. 6; 11. 6.25; 12. 79.

8 • Plan a Schedule Computation and Mental Math

Objective: Students will solve problems by adding and subtracting fractions and mixed numbers. They will practice adding mixed numbers using $\frac{1}{4}$ and $\frac{1}{2}$.

Materials:

• *Grab-and-Go!™ Teacher Guide and Activity Resources,* Four-Column Chart, p. 39, (1 per student)

Answers: Sample answer: Week 1: Exercise, Yard work at home, Reading, Clean room:

$2\frac{1}{2} + 1\frac{1}{4} + 1\frac{3}{4} + 1\frac{1}{4} = 6\frac{3}{4}$; Week 2: Yard work for Mrs. Carlson, Math, Recycling:

$2\frac{1}{4} + 2\frac{1}{3} + 1\frac{1}{4} = 5\frac{5}{6}$.

8 • Mixed Measures Geometry and Measurement

Objective: Students will practice using rulers to model adding mixed numbers that include $\frac{1}{2}$, $\frac{1}{4}$, and $\frac{1}{8}$. They will model and solve fraction addition problems using a measured line.

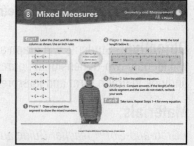

Materials:

• *Grab-and-Go!™ Teacher Guide and Activity Resources,* Two-Column Chart, p. 37, (1 per student)

• Inch ruler, a blue and a green marker or color pencil (1 per student)

Answers: 1. $3\frac{1}{8}$; 2. $5\frac{3}{4}$; 3. $5\frac{7}{8}$; 4. $4\frac{1}{4}$; 5. $5\frac{3}{8}$; 6. 3.

8 • Pattern Block Mix-Up Challenge

Objective: Students will solve addition and subtraction problems with fractions and mixed numbers and express answers in simplest form. They will write and solve fraction equations from pictorial cards and match their results to equation cards based on the simplified fraction answer.

Materials:

• *Grab-and-Go!™ Teacher Guide and Activity Resources,* Three-Column Chart, p. 38 (1 per student); Pattern Block Equation Cards, p. 63 (1 per pair)

Answers: $1\frac{1}{4} + 1\frac{2}{4} = 2\frac{3}{4}$; $1\frac{1}{2} + 1\frac{1}{2} = 3$; $1\frac{1}{4} + 1\frac{2}{4} = 2\frac{3}{4}$; $2\frac{4}{5} + 1\frac{3}{5} = 4\frac{2}{5}$; $2\frac{3}{6} + \frac{5}{6} = 3\frac{1}{3}$;

$2\frac{2}{6} + 3\frac{2}{3} = 6$; $1\frac{1}{3} + 2\frac{1}{2} = 3\frac{5}{6}$; $2\frac{2}{4} + 2\frac{1}{2} = 5$.

9 • State Stats Computation and Mental Math

Objective: Students will graph a given set of data using a bar graph. They will use the population of a state for three different years to make a bar graph showing data.

Materials:

• *Grab-and-Go!™ Teacher Guide and Activity Resources,* Four-Column Chart, p.39 (1 per student); State Populations worksheet, p. 64 (1 per student); Centimeter Grid, p. 59 (1 per student)

Answers: Anticipated outcomes: Students' graphs should have an appropriate scale for their data, and the data should be accurately represented. Axes and graphs should have titles.

9 • Capital Temperatures Geometry and Measurement

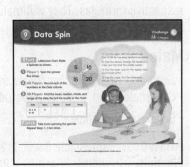

Objective: Students will graph a given set of data using a bar graph. They will use average monthly temperatures to create a bar graph.

Materials:

• *Grab-and-Go!™ Teacher Guide and Activity Resources,* Two-Column Chart, p. 37 (1 per student); State Capital Temperature worksheet, p. 65 (1 per student); Centimeter Grid, p. 59 (1 per student)

Answers: Anticipated outcomes: Students' graphs should have an appropriate scale for their data, and the data should be accurately represented. Axes and graphs should have titles.

9 • Data Spin Challenge

Objective: Students will describe characteristics of data including median, mode, and range. They will use numbers from a spinner to find mean, median, mode, and range of data.

Materials:

• *Grab-and-Go!™ Teacher Guide and Activity Resources,* Five-Column Chart, p. 40 (1 per student); Circle/Spinner, p. 47 (1 per group)

• Transparent spinner

Answers: Sample answers: Data: 10, 20, 10, 5, 10; Mean: 11; Median: 10; Mode: 10; Range: 20 − 5 = 15.

10 • Awesome Areas Computation and Mental Math

Objective: Students will select and use appropriate units and formulas to measure area. They will find, estimate, and measure the faces of objects to find the areas of each.

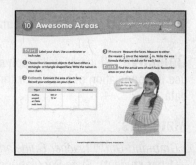

Materials:

- *Grab-and-Go!™ Teacher Guide and Activity Resources,* Four-Column Chart, p. 39 (1 per student)
- Centimeter or inch ruler

Answers: Sample answers: Object: paper; Estimate; 80 in.²; Formula: $8\frac{1}{2} \times 11$; Actual Area: 93.5 in.² Object: pennant; Estimate: 50 in.²; Formula $\frac{1}{2} \times 6 \times 12$; Actual Area: 36 in.²

10 • Triangle Trials Geometry and Measurement

Objective: Students will select and use appropriate units and formulas to measure area. They will compare areas of a rectangle, two triangles, and a parallelogram made from the same original shape.

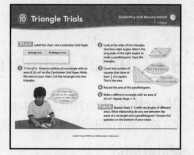

Materials:

- *Grab-and-Go!™ Teacher Guide and Activity Resources,* Three-Column Chart, p. 38; Centimeter Grid, p. 59 (1 per student)
- Scissors

Answers: Sample answer: The area of a triangle is $\frac{1}{2}$ the area of the rectangle from which it came. The area of a parallelogram is equal to the area of a rectangle with the same base and height.

10 • Fabulous Formulas Challenge

Objective: Students will connect models for perimeter and area with their respective formulas. They will match expressions with correct models for finding area or perimeter of rectangles.

Materials:

- *Grab-and-Go!™ Teacher Guide and Activity Resources,* Two-Column Chart, p. 37; Centimeter Grid, p. 59 (1 per student)
- Scissors, glue stick

Answers: Expression: 5 × 7; 2(2) + 2(6); 2(4 + 7); 3 × 3; 1 × 9 Formula: length × width; 2(length) + 2(width); 2(length) + 2(width); length × width; Perimeter: (second row) 18; (third row) 22; Area: (first row) 35 cm²; (fourth row) 9 cm²; (fifth row) 9 cm². Models should match expressions.

11 • Special 5 Computation and Mental Math

Objective: Students will use multiplication to solve problems involving whole numbers and estimate products of two-digit by two-digit multiplication. Students use arrays to solve two-digit by two-digit multiplication problems.

Materials:

• *Grab-and-Go!™ Teacher Guide and Activity Resources,* Five-Column Chart, p. 40 (1 per student); Centimeter Grid, p. 59 (3 per student); Circle/Spinner, p. 47 (1 per student)

Answers: Sample answer: 35 × 45 = 1,575; 40 × 50 = 2,000; 30 × 40 = 1,200; 30 × 50 = 1,500; 40 × 40 = 1,600.

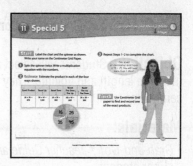

11 • Amazing Areas Geometry and Measurement

Objective: Students will multiply to solve measurement problems involving length, width, and area.

Materials:

• *Grab-and-Go!™ Teacher Guide and Activity Resources,* Four-Column Chart, p. 39 (1 per student)

• Inch ruler and objects to measure (suggested objects: box of tissues, textbook, board eraser, box of crayons)

Answers: Sample answer: Window: 32 in. × 27 in. = 864 in.²

11 • Multiplication Relay Challenge

Objective: Students will multiply to solve meaningful problems. They practice multiplying by two-digit numbers.

Materials:

• *Grab-and-Go!™ Teacher Guide and Activity Resources,* Computation Recording Sheet, p. 66; Two-Digit Times Two-Digit Multiplication Mat, p. 67 (1 per student)

• Number Cards 0–9 (two sets), p. 69, or number tiles 0–9 (two sets); calculator or multiplication chart

Answers: Sample answer: 27 × 31 = 837.

12 • Inner Space Computation and Mental Math

Objective: Students will select and use appropriate units and formulas to measure length and volume. They will find the volume of rectangular prisms using a centimeter ruler.

Materials:

- *Grab-and-Go!™ Teacher Guide and Activity Resources,* Six-Column Chart, p. 41 (1 per student)
- Centimeter ruler, classroom objects that are rectangular prisms (book, box of tissues, box of paper clips, lunch box, box of markers, eraser)

Answers: Anticipated outcome: Volumes should equal length × width × height.

12 • What's in the Box? Geometry and Measurement

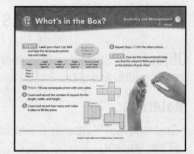

Objective: Students will find the volume of rectangular prisms by using unit cubes as models. They will estimate the volume of prisms by stacking unit cubes into nets that have been folded to make prisms.

Materials:

- *Grab-and-Go!™ Teacher Guide and Activity Resources,* Five-Column Chart, p. 40 (1 per student); Prism Nets, p. 68 (1 per pair)
- 50-piece unit cube set, scissors, tape

Answers: Prism 1: Length: 3, Width: 3, Height: 3, Volume: 27; Prism 2: Length: 2, Width: 6, Height: 2, Volume: 24; Prism 3: Length: 2, Width: 3, Height: 4, Volume: 24; Sample Answer: Length times width times height equals volume.

12 • It's in the Can! Challenge

Objective: Students will estimate the volume of a cylinder by estimating the number of unit cubes that will fit inside the cylinder.

Materials:

- *Grab-and-Go!™ Teacher Guide and Activity Resources,* Four-Column Chart, p. 39; Centimeter Grid, p. 59 (1 per student)
- 50-piece unit cube set, three cylinders of varying sizes

Answers: Anticipated outcome: Estimated volumes should be based on number of unit cubes used in measuring the base and height of cylinder.

13 • Dueling Decimals Computation and Mental Math

Objective: Students will multiply with decimals. They will make decimal multiplication problems that involve zeros.

Materials:

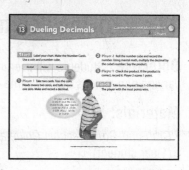

- *Grab-and-Go!™ Teacher Guide and Activity Resources,* Three-Column Chart, p. 38 (1 per student); Number Cards 1–14, p. 69 (1 per pair)
- Scissors, counter labeled 00 and 0, Number Cube Patterns, p. 107, or number cube labeled 1–6, coin

Answers: Sample answer: 3.002 × 8 = 24.016

13 • Market Multiplication Geometry and Measurement

Objective: Students will multiply with decimals. They will multiply the price per pound (decimals as a money amount) by the number of pounds (in decimals). Then they will find the total cost of a purchase of fruits and vegetables.

Materials:

- *Grab-and-Go!™ Teacher Guide and Activity Resources,* Four-Column Chart, p. 39, (1 per student)
- Number Cube Patterns, p. 107, or number cube labeled 0–5 and number cube labeled 1–6

Answers: Sample answer: 5.2 × $3.76 = $19.55

13 • Tic-Tac-Decimals Challenge

Objective: Students will practice estimating and finding the product of two decimal numbers. Then they will write and solve decimal multiplication problems to check their estimate.

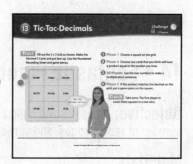

Materials:

- *Grab-and-Go!™ Teacher Guide and Activity Resources,* 3 × 3 Grid, p. 55 (1 per pair); Computation Recording Sheet, p. 66, (1 per student); Decimal Cards 3, p. 70 (1 per pair)
- Scissors, counters or cubes (1 per pair)

Answers: Sample answers: 8.256 = 1.72 × 4.8; 19.488 = 4.8 × 4.06; 78.72 = 4.8 × 16.4; 47.424 = 9.88 × 4.8; 401.128 = 40.6 × 9.88; 66.584 = 16.4 × 4.06; 6.9832 = 4.06 × 1.72; 100.32 = 4.8 × 20.9

14 • Vary the Volume Computation and Mental Math

Objective: Students will use unit cubes to build rectangular prisms with varying dimensions but the same volume.

Materials:

• *Grab-and-Go!™ Teacher Guide and Activity Resources,* Four-Column Chart, p. 39 (1 per student)

• 36 unit cubes

Answers: Sample answer: length: 4 cubes; width: 3 cubes; height: 3 cubes; volume: 36 cubic units.

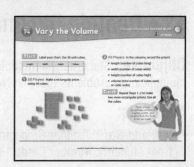

14 • 3-D Construction Geometry and Measurement

Objective: Students will build a cube, a triangular pyramid, and a square pyramid and identify the number of faces, edges, and vertices on each.

Materials:

• *Grab-and-Go!™ Teacher Guide and Activity Resources,* Four-Column Chart, p. 39; Cube Net, p. 71; Triangular Pyramid Net, p. 72; Square Pyramid Net, p. 73 (1 per student)

• Scissors, glue or tape

Answers: cube: 6 faces, 12 edges, 8 vertices; triangular pyramid: 4 faces, 6 edges, 4 vertices; square pyramid: 5 faces, 8 edges, 5 vertices.

14 • Fantastic Figures Challenge

Objective: Students will build an octahedron and a dodecahedron and record the number of faces, edges, and vertices on each figure.

Materials:

• *Grab-and-Go!™ Teacher Guide and Activity Resources,* Four-Column Chart, p. 39; Octahedron Net, p. 74; Dodecahedron Net, p. 75 (1 per student)

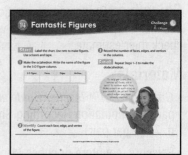

Answers: octahedron: 8 faces (equilateral triangles), 12 edges, 6 vertices; dodecahedron: 12 faces (pentagons), 30 edges, 20 vertices

15 • Divide and Conquer Computation and Mental Math

Objective: Students will use number cubes and a spinner to make and divide problems with three-digit dividends by two-digit divisors.

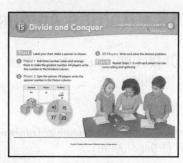

Materials:

• *Grab-and-Go!™ Teacher Guide and Activity Resources,* Three-Column Chart, p. 38 (1 per student); Circle/Spinner, p. 47 (1 per group)

• Transparent spinner, Number Cube Patterns, p. 107, or three number cubes labeled 1–6

Answers: Sample answer: $23\overline{)641}$ = 27 R20

15 • 15-Minute March Geometry and Measurement

Objective: Students find how many 15-minute time increments are in a given length of time. They will write and solve division problems to match the situation.

Materials:

• *Grab-and-Go!™ Teacher Guide and Activity Resources,* Four-Column Chart, p. 39 (1 per student); Division Story Cards, p. 76 (1 per group)

• Brass fastener, scissors

Answers: 1. $45 ÷ 15 = 3$; 2. $30 ÷ 15 = 2$; 3. $75 ÷ 15 = 5$; 4. $90 ÷ 15 = 6$; 5. $195 ÷ 15 = 13$; 6. $150 ÷ 15 = 10$; 7. $60 ÷ 15 = 4$; 8. $300 ÷ 15 = 20$.

15 • Decide and Divide Challenge

Objective: Students choose their dividends and divisors and then estimate quotients, dividing three-digit dividends by two-digit divisors.

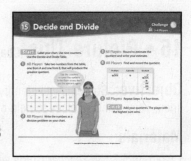

Materials:

• *Grab-and-Go!™ Teacher Guide and Activity Resources,* Three-Column Chart, p. 38 (1 per student); Decide and Divide Table, p. 77 (1 per group)

• 9 counters

Answers: Sample answer: $828 ÷ 18 = 46$

16 • Rolling Angles Computation and Mental Math

Objective: Students will draw angles using a protractor and then classify the angles.

Materials:

• *Grab-and-Go!™ Teacher Guide and Activity Resources,* Three-Column Chart p. 38 (1 per student)

• Protractor Pattern, p. 109, or protractor; Number Cube Patterns, p. 107

Answers: Sample answers: 124°: obtuse; 90°: right; 44°: acute; 180°: straight

16 • Geometry MATHO Geometry and Measurement

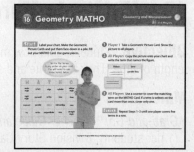

Objective: Students will match geometric drawings with their terms. They will match pictures of shapes on Geometry Picture Cards with the correct term written on a MATHO Card.

Materials:

• *Grab-and-Go!™ Teacher Guide and Activity Resources,* Two-Column Chart p. 37, (1 per student); MATHO Card, p. 43; Geometric Picture Cards, p. 78 (1 per group)

• Two-sided counters

Answers: Sample answer: vertex

16 • Picture This Challenge

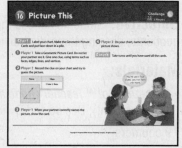

Objective: Students will identify and describe attributes of geometric shapes and lines. They will give clues to help other students identify shapes or lines.

Materials:

• *Grab-and-Go!™ Teacher Guide and Activity Resources,* Two-Column Chart, p. 37 (1 per student); Geometric Picture Cards, p. 78 (1 per pair)

Answers: Sample clue: This solid has 6 faces and 8 vertices. The shape of this solid's base is a square. Each face of this solid is a rectangle. Answer: The shape is a rectangular prism.

17 • D is for... Computation and Mental Math

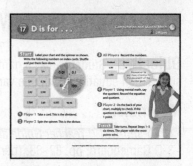

Objective: Students will divide using decimals. They will use decimal cards and a spinner to make and solve decimal division equations.

Materials:

- *Grab-and-Go!™ Teacher Guide and Activity Resources,* Four-Column Chart, p. 39 (1 per student); Circle/Spinner, p. 47 (1 per pair)
- Ten index cards, transparent spinner

Answers: Sample answer: $3.56 \div 100 = 0.0356$

17 • Centimeter Division Geometry and Measurement

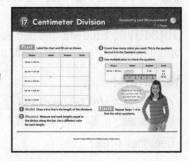

Objective: Students will divide with decimals and verify the reasonableness of the results. They will draw and divide line segments to solve problems involving the division of decimal numbers by whole numbers.

Materials:

- *Grab-and-Go!™ Teacher Guide and Activity Resources,* Four-Column Chart, p. 39 (1 per student)
- Color pencils or markers (six colors)

Answers: 3; 7; 5; 6; 4

17 • Grid It Challenge

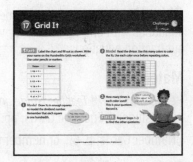

Objective: Students will divide using decimals. They will use grids to make models showing division of a decimal number by another decimal number.

Materials:

- *Grab-and-Go!™ Teacher Guide and Activity Resources,* Two-Column Chart, p. 37 (1 per student); Hundredths Grid p. 79, (2 per student)
- Crayons or colored markers

Answers: 0.2; 0.4; 0.02; 0.3; 0.05; 0.3

18 • Mental Math Moves Computation and Mental Math

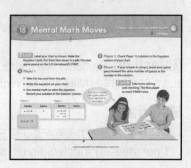

Objective: Students play a game by using mental math to solve addition and subtraction equations with one variable.

Materials:

• *Grab-and-Go!™ Teacher Guide and Activity Resources,* Equation Cards, pp. 80–81; 3-D Gameboard, pp. 82–83, (per group); Two-Column Chart, p. 37 (per student)

• 2 game pieces

Answers: $a = 5$; $b = 7$; $c = 6$; $d = 4$; $e = 2$; $f = 3$; $g = 7$; $h = 6$; $j = 9$; $k = 5$; $l = 4$; $m = 8$; $n = 2$; $p = 7$; $q = 3$; $r = 1$; $s = 4$; $t = 9$; $u = 1$; $v = 3$; $w = 5$; $x = 2$; $y = 8$; $z = 4$

18 • What's Missing? Geometry and Measurement

Objective: Students will use addition and subtraction equations to find the length of one side of an irregular polygon.

Materials:

• *Grab-and-Go!™ Teacher Guide and Activity Resources,* What's Missing? Worksheet, p. 84 (per student)

• Centimeter ruler

Answers: 1. $19 - x = 13$, $13 + x = 19$, $x = 6$ 2. $24 - z = 19$, $19 + z = 24$, $z = 5$ 3. $9 - y = 7$, $7 + y = 9$, $y = 2$ 4. $19 - t = 14$, $14 + t = 19$, $t = 5$ 5. $20 - v = 15$, $15 + v = 20$, $v = 5$ 6. $20 - m = 17$, $17 + m = 20$, $m = 3$

18 • Tell Me a Story Challenge

Objective: Students will use mental math to solve addition and subtraction equations with one variable. They will write story problems that match addition and subtraction equations.

Materials:

• *Grab-and-Go!™ Teacher Guide and Activity Resources,* Three-Column Chart, p. 38; (per student) Equation Cards, pp. 80–81 (per group)

• Number Cards, p. 69, or number tiles

Answers: $a = 5$; $b = 7$; $c = 6$; $d = 4$; $e = 2$; $f = 3$; $g = 7$; $h = 6$; $j = 9$; $k = 5$; $l = 4$; $m = 8$; $n = 2$; $p = 7$; $q = 3$; $r = 1$; $s = 4$; $t = 9$; $u = 1$; $v = 3$; $w = 5$; $x = 2$; $y = 8$; $z = 4$; Students' story problems should match the equations.

19 • Let's Shake! Computation and Mental Math

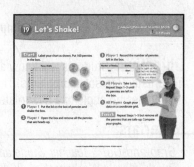

Objective: Students will describe the relationship between sets of data in tables. They will make a table from data collected by shaking pennies in a box and removing all the heads-up pennies.

Materials:

- *Grab-and-Go!™ Teacher Guide and Activity Resources,* Two-column Chart, p. 37 (1 per student)
- 100 pennies, box with secure lid

Answers: Anticipated outcome: After each toss, about half the pennies should be heads-up, leaving about half still in the box.

19 • Figure Out the Points Geometry and Measurement

Objective: Students will recognize the connection between ordered pairs of numbers and locations of points on a plane. They will map ordered pairs on a coordinate grid to find letters that spell the name of a figure outlined by points on the grid.

Materials:

- *Grab-and-Go!™ Teacher Guide and Activity Resources,* Coordinate Figure Worksheet, p. 85 (1 per student)

Answers: (3, 6)E (5, 3)N (5, 8)T (7, 3)O (3, 3)P (7, 6)G (6, 7)A (4, 7)N; pentagon

19 • What's the Point? Challenge

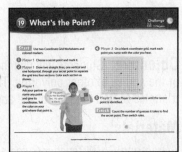

Objective: Students will recognize the connection between ordered pairs of numbers and locations of points on a plane. They will graph ordered pairs and try to locate a specific ordered pair using the guess-and-check method.

Materials:

- *Grab-and-Go!™ Teacher Guide and Activity Resources,* Coordinate Planes, p. 112; Centimeter Grid, p. 59 (1 per student)
- Crayons or markers

Answers: Anticipated outcome: Students should be able to gather enough data to determine the secret point marked on a coordinate grid.

20 • 360° Sums Computation and Mental Math

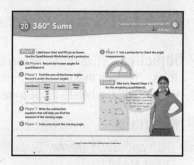

Objective: Students will know and use the sum of the angles of a quadrilateral to solve problems. They will use the measures of three angles to find a missing angle of a quadrilateral.

Materials:

• *Grab-and-Go!™ Teacher Guide and Activity Resources,* Four-Column Chart, p. 39; Quadrilaterals Worksheet, p. 86 (1 per student)

• Protractor Pattern, p. 109, or protractor

Answers: A: 105°; B: 203°; C: 90°; D: 113°; E: 103°; F: 192°

20 • Protractor Practice Geometry and Measurement

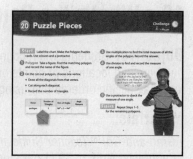

Objective: Students will practice using a protractor to measure angles. They will use a protractor to measure all three angles of given triangles. They will then classify each triangle according to its angles.

Materials:

• *Grab-and-Go!™ Teacher Guide and Activity Resources,* Five-Column Chart, p. 40; Triangles Worksheet, p. 87 (1 per student)

• Protractor Pattern, p. 109, or protractor

Answers: A: 43°, 90°, 47°, right; B: 34°, 24°, 122°, obtuse; C: 60°, 60°, 60°, acute; D: 90°, 27°, 63°, right; E: 80°, 55°, 45°, acute; F: 108°, 44°, 28°, obtuse

20 • Puzzle Pieces Challenge

Objective: Students will use the sum of the angles of a triangle to find the sum of the angles of other polygons. They will cut polygons into triangles and use the triangles to find the sum of the angles of the whole polygon.

Materials:

• *Grab-and-Go!™ Teacher Guide and Activity Resources,* Four-Column Chart, p. 39; Polygon Puzzles Cards, p. 88 (1 per student)

• scissors, ruler, Protractor Pattern, p. 109, or protractor

Answers: Triangle: 180°, 60°; rectangle: 360°, 90°; pentagon: 540°, 108°; hexagon: 720°, 120°; octagon: 1,080°, 135°; decagon: 1, 440°, 144°

1 • Prime or Composite?

Objective: To classify numbers as prime or composite.

Materials: *For partners* 29 slips of paper, paper bag, 30 counters, pencil, paper, 2 different coins

Playing the Game: This activity reinforces students' understanding of prime and composite numbers. It also provides students with an opportunity to create arrays that model multiplication facts with products less than 31.

In preparing for the game, players label slips of paper with numbers 2 through 30. They place the slips in a bag and shake it up. The first player draws a slip and classifies the number as either prime or composite. If the number drawn is composite, the player then uses the counters to make as many arrays as possible. When the first player is finished, the second player can create an array that has not been identified, if any.

Players use the coins as counters and move ahead 2 spaces for each prime number drawn.

They move 1 space for each array created. The player to reach *Finish* first wins the game.

2 • Savings Account

Objective: To calculate percents of 2-digit numbers.

Materials: *For players* 10 index cards, Number Cube Patterns, p.107, or 2 number cubes (1–6), paper and pencil

Playing the Game: This activity reinforces students' ability to calculate a percent of a number. In preparation for the activity, students label 10 index cards with specified percents. They shuffle the cards and place them facedown in a stack. Students also make score cards for recording their scores after each round.

The game begins when the first player rolls the number cubes to form a two-digit number. The result of the first roll is the ones digit. Player 1 then draws a percent card and calculates that percent of the number. The number and percent, expressed in dollars and cents, is recorded on the score card. Player 2 then rolls the number cubes and repeats the process. The player with the greater savings total after five rounds is the winner.

3 • Ride the Course

Objective: To add and subtract decimals.

Materials: *For partners* Decimal Addition and Subtraction Cards pp. 110-111, 3-Section Spinner p. 92, 2 different counters, calculator

Playing the Game: This activity provides students with an opportunity to reinforce their ability adding and subtracting decimals. Students prepare for the activity by shuffling the addition and subtraction cards and placing them facedown in a pile. Students also select counters to use as game pieces and place them on *Start*.

The game begins as the first player draws a card from the pile. The player gives the solution to the problem. The other player uses a calculator to check the answer. If correct, the first player spins the spinner and moves his or her game piece according to the result of the spin. The second player then draws a card from the pile and repeats the process. The first player to reach *Finish* wins the game.

4 • What's the Difference?

Objective: To subtract fractions with unlike denominators.

Materials: *For partners* Four sets of Number Cards (1–8), p. 69, paper and pencils

Playing the Game: This activity reinforces students' understanding of subtraction of fractions with unlike denominators. Students prepare for the activity by drawing a problem outline on a sheet of paper.

The game begins as one player shuffles the number cards and deals four cards to each player. Players use their cards to create two fractions with the least possible difference. They display their fractions by placing the cards on their problem outlines. Players then solve one another's subtraction problems to determine the fraction pair with the least difference. They player who formed this pair scores 1 point. The first player to score 5 points wins the game.

5 • Mean of Means

Objective: To practice finding mean

Materials: *For players* Number Cube Patterns, p. 107, or number cube (labeled even numbers 6–16), 18 red and 18 blue connecting cubes or counters

Playing the Game: This activity gives students an opportunity to practice finding the mean. The first player rolls the number cube 2 times and uses connecting cubes to model each number. The student should use the red cubes for one number and the blue cubes for the other number. If the stacks have an equal number of cubes, the student should record the number of one of the stacks as the mean. If stacks are not equal, the student should make them equal by moving cubes from the taller stack to the shorter stack. The next player will repeat the process.

After the fifth round, players will find the mean for rounds 1–5 using computation. The player with the greater mean for rounds 1–5 is the winner.

6 • Picture Problems

Objective: To subtract mixed numbers and fractions with unlike denominators.

Materials: *For players* 16 index cards, crayons or markers, drawing paper

Playing the Game: This activity reinforces students' ability to subtract mixed numbers and fractions with unlike denominators. Students prepare for the activity by labeling index cards with specified mixed numbers and fractions. The labeled cards are then shuffled and placed facedown in a stack.

The game begins as one player takes two cards and draws a picture to illustrate the subtraction sentence formed from the result. The other players observe the picture and solve the subtraction sentence it represents. Players who identify the correct difference receive 1 point. The next player takes two new cards from the pile and repeats the process. When all cards have been drawn, the player with the greatest number of points wins the game. If there is a tie, the cards are reshuffled and restacked. Play continues until the tie is broken.

7 • Decimal Challenge

Objective: To practice comparing and ordering decimals.

Materials: *For each player* symbol cards labeled <, >, =, game piece; *For partners* Number Cube Patterns, p. 107, or number cube labeled 1, 1, 1, 2, 2, 3

Playing the Game: This activity provides students with an opportunity to practice comparing and ordering decimals. Players take turns rolling a number cube and advancing their game pieces according to the results. Each time a game piece is moved, the player draws a symbol card. Depending on the card, the player names a decimal greater than, less than, or equal to the decimal on which he or she landed. If the decimal named does not fit the criterion, the player loses a turn. The first player to reach *FINISH* wins.

8 • Fraction Factors

Objective: To multiply fractions.

Materials: *For players* 3 sets of number cards (1–9), score chart, paper and pencils

Playing the Game: This activity reinforces students' ability to multiply fractions. Students prepare for the activity by making game boards used to organize multiplication sentences with fraction factors. They also make a score chart for recording their scores.

The game begins as the number cards are shuffled and placed face down in a stack. The first player draws 4 cards and forms fraction factors that yield the greatest possible product. The player places the cards on the game board. The second player finds the product and records it in the scoring table. The second player then draws four new cards and repeats the process. At the end of each round, players compare the products of their problems. The player with the greater product earns 1 point. The first player to accumulate 5 points wins the game.

9 • Just Checking

Objective: To add and subtract whole numbers extending through the millions place.

Materials: *For each player* paper and pencil; *For players* 12 index cards

Playing the Game: This activity reinforces students' ability to add and subtract whole numbers extending to the millions place. In preparing for the game, each player writes four-, five-, six-, and seven-digit numbers on four index cards. The cards are collected, shuffled, and placed face down in a stack.

The game begins when Player 1 turns over the top two cards and finds their sum. The other players use subtraction to check that the answer is correct. If so, Player 1 earns one point. Player 2 then turns over the next two cards and repeats the process. When the stack is depleted, the cards are reshuffled and placed in a new stack. Round 2 begins with play continuing in the same manner.

At the end of Round 2, the cards are again reshuffled and restacked. For Rounds 3 and 4, the players find the difference of the cards drawn and the answer is checked through addition. At the end of four rounds, the player with the greatest point total wins the game.

10 • It's a Toss-Up

Objective: To graph ordered pairs on a coordinate grid.

Materials: *For players* 10 beanbags, Centimeter Grid, p. 59, or large coordinate grid

Playing the Game: This activity reinforces students' understanding of ordered pairs and the coordinate grid. As the game begins, the first player stands at the start location and attempts to throw the 10 beanbags onto the large grid. The other player expresses the results of the tosses as an ordered pair with the first number representing the round and the second number representing the number of bags that landed on the large grid. That player then graphs this ordered pair on a coordinate grid. Then players switch roles.

After 4 rounds, the players connect the points with lines. The players analyze the results and determine how to identify the winner.

11 • Powerful Products

Objective: To multiply decimals.

Materials: *For players* Number Cards (0–9), p. 69, decimal product outline, calculator, chart, paper bag, paper

Playing the Game: This activity provides students with an opportunity to reinforce their ability to multiply decimal factors. Students prepare for the activity by making a decimal product outline that will be used to display multiplication sentences. They also make a three-column chart for recording their scores and points.

The game begins as the number cards are placed in a paper bag. After shaking the bag, the first player draws four cards. The player uses the cards to create two decimal factors that will yield the greatest possible product. The player displays these decimal factors on the outline and identifies their product. The second player uses the calculator to check the answer. If correct, the product is recorded in the scoring chart. If incorrect, a zero is recorded. The cards are then returned to the bag. Players trade roles and repeat the process. At the end of the round, the player who formed a multiplication sentence with the greater product earns 1 point. The first player to accumulate 5 points wins the game.

12 • Patterns in Play

Objective: To practice extending patterns.

Materials: *For players* colored tiles, paper bag

Playing the Game: This activity provides students with an opportunity to practice extending patterns. One player will create a pattern unit of 5 tiles. Then players will each draw 5 tiles from the bag. The next player will try to continue the pattern with one of his or her tiles. If the second player does not have the tile, then he or she should draw tiles from the bag until able to do so. Play continues until the bag is empty and a player cannot continue the pattern. The player with fewest tiles left is the winner.

13 • What's Left?

Objective: To understand how a remainder affects division problems

Materials: *For players* 2 sets of 10 different-colored counters

Playing the Game: This game reinforces students' understanding of division with remainders. In preparing for the game, each player receives a set of 10 counters.

Player 1 chooses a number from 1 to 20. This number will be the remainder for the round. Player 2 will write a division problem that will give a quotient with the remainder that was stated by Player 1. Player 1 will check the division problem. If it is correct, Player 2 places a counter on the card on the board that corresponds to the remainder. If incorrect, Player 1 places his or her counter on that card.

Players reverse roles for the next round. Students should choose remainders that have not been chosen yet. After 10 rounds, the player with the greater number of counters wins.

14 • Predicting Sums

Objective: To list all possible outcomes of a probability experiment and predict outcomes based on the list.

Materials: *For partners* Number Cube Patterns, p. 107, or number cubes labeled 1–6, Tally Table, p. 108, paper and pencil

Playing the Game: In this activity, students predict how often a particular sum will occur when two number cubes are tossed and their results are added. Prior to beginning the game, the group lists all the combinations of addends that are possible from the number cubes. Each player analyzes the list and predicts the sum that will occur most often and the sum that will occur least often when the cubes are tossed 40 times. Players record their predictions on paper. They also create a tally table for recording their data.

Players then take turns tossing the cubes, finding the sum displayed, and recording the result. After 40 tosses, the sum that occurred most often and the sum that occurred least often are identified. Players reveal their predictions. The player who correctly predicted which sums occur most and least often wins the game.

15 • Match Up

Objective: To divide decimals.

Materials: *For partners* Match Up Cards (Division, Compatible numbers, and Estimate cards), p. 113

Playing the Game: This activity provides students with an opportunity to reinforce their ability to divide decimals and estimate products. In preparing for the game, students shuffle the division cards and place them face-down in a 3-by-4 array. They do the same for the compatible number cards and the estimate cards, making a separate array with each type of card.

The game begins as the first player turns over a card from each array. If the cards match, the player picks them up and goes again. It the cards do not match, they are returned to their original positions, and the next player goes. Play continues in this manner until all cards have been picked up. The player holding the greater number of cards wins the game.

16 • 2 Steps Forward, 1 Step Back

Objective: To practice changing customary and metric units

Materials: *For players* game pieces, Customary and Metric Game Cards, p. 117

Playing the Game: This activity gives students an opportunity to practice changing customary and metric units. Players shuffle the game cards and place them facedown in a pile. Players will then place their game pieces on START. Player 1 will draw a card from the pile, read it, and decide whether it is true or false. Player 2 will check the answer.

If correct, Player 1 moves 2 steps forward on the board. If incorrect, Player 1 will move 1 step back on the board, or remain at START. Students will reverse roles and continue until one student reaches FINISH.

17 • What's Your Angle?

Objective: To practice comparing and ordering decimals.

Materials: *For partners* Protractor Pattern, p.109, or protractors, scoring table, paper and pencil

Playing the Game: This activity provides students with an opportunity to practice drawing and measuring angles. Prior to beginning the activity, players create a scoring table for recording their measurements.

The game begins as Player 1 draws an angle. Player 2 observes the drawing and predicts the angle's measure. Using a protractor, Player 2 measures the angle and records the actual measure. Players determine the difference between the actual measure and the predicted measure and record the value.

Players trade roles and repeat the process. After five rounds, the player with the lower score wins the game.

18 • Around the Block

Objective: To find the perimeter of closed figures.

Materials: *For players* 2 different-color counters, 3-Section Spinner, p. 92, labeled 1–3, Centimeter Grid, p. 59, or graph paper, pencils

Playing the Game: This activity reinforces students' understanding of perimeter. As the game begins, students place their game pieces on the *Start* square.

Player 1 spins the spinner and moves his or her game piece according to the result of the spin. The player then draws as many rectangles as possible that have the perimeter labeled at the game piece's new location. The player receives 1 point for each rectangle drawn. Player 2 then spins the spinner and repeats the process. When both game pieces have completed one trip around the board, the player with the greater point total wins the game.

19 • Model Makers

Objective: To identify the traits of geometric plane figures and construct the figures concretely.

Materials: *For players* toothpicks, 24 slips of paper, container

Playing the Game: This activity reinforces students' understanding of the traits of plane figures. Prior to playing the game, each student writes an "I am" clue for six different plane figures. The clues are placed in a container.

The game begins when the first player draws a clue and reads it aloud. The second player listens to the clue and makes a toothpick model of the plane figure described. If the model is correct, the second player earns one point. If the model is incorrect, the third player can steal the point by making the correct model. The second player then draws a new slip, and the process is repeated while the players trade roles. When all slips have been drawn, the player with the greatest point total wins the game.

20 • Triple Play

Objective: To find the perimeter of closed figures.

Materials: *For players* Number Cube Patterns, p. 107, or three number cubes each labeled 2, 2, 3, 3, 4, 4; 64 cube blocks, paper and pencil

Playing the Game: This activity reinforces students' understanding of volume. Prior to beginning the activity, each player creates a score chart.

The game begins as Player 1 tosses three number cubes and records the results in the chart. These represent the length, width, and height of a rectangular prism. The player then calculates the volume of the prism. If correct, Player 1 receives one point. An additional point can be earned if the player constructs a rectangular prism made from cube blocks that has the same volume. Player 2 then rolls the number cubes and repeats the process. After 10 rounds, the player with the greater score wins the game.

100% Trivia About Money
by Herbert E. Ellis

Focus: percents

Story Summary: *100% Trivia About Money* provides many fun facts about United States currency that involve percentages.

Vocabulary: percent, fraction, percentage

Responding Answers:
1. 5%
2. A 5-cent note is 1/20 of a dollar, or 5%; a 25-cent note is 1/4 of a dollar, or 25%.
3. 10%; 60%
Activity 1. None; the notes are not paper. They are made of cotton and linen that come from plants. 2. It is 1/4, or 1 quarter of a dollar. 3. Sample answers: Keep it and begin collecting old money; display it under glass; sell it to a collector.
4. Answers will vary.

A Hundredth of a Second
by H. J. Laager

Focus: adding and subtracting decimals

Story Summary: *A Hundredth of a Second* describes Olympic events in which competitors' times are just tenths or hundredths of a second apart.

Vocabulary: decimal, tenth, hundredth, fraction

Responding Answers:
1. You subtract the first-place time from the third-place time to find their difference.
2. 0.78 of a second; 0.58 + 0.2 = 0.78 3. 57.22; 57.89 − 0.67 = 57.22
Activity Students add and subtract decimal numbers between 1.00 and 10.00.

A Math Mix-Up
by Stephanie Herbek

Focus: metric vs. customary measurement

Story Summary: NASA's Mars Climate Orbiter crashed into Mars in September 1999 because of a mix-up in customary vs. metric units used in the calculations of the approach to and orbit of the planet.

Vocabulary: kilometer, meter, centimeter, mile, yard, inch, standard system of measurement, metric system

Responding Answers:
1. the standard system 2. the kilometer 3. Sample Answer: NASA uses standard units when they share information, because in America, most things are measured in standard units. Americans are more familiar with this system of measurement.
4. 10.16 cm
Activity Check students' estimates and totals.

A Roller Coaster of Angles
by Carter W. Ryan

Focus: angles and lines

Story Summary: *A Roller Coaster of Angles* explains some of the history behind roller coasters and how geometry plays a role in these popular rides.

Vocabulary: angle, acute angle, degrees, parallel lines, perpendicular, right angle, obtuse angle

Responding Answers:
1. Coaster B would pick up more speed. It has a steeper angle.
2.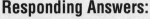

3. Answers should describe angles, paths, and shapes of favorite roller coasters.
Activity Students design a roller coaster and a flyer about the ride that includes height, speed, materials, and angle of descent.

And the Survey Says
by Megan Hill, illustrated by Alan Flinn

Focus: relating fractions and decimals and help support student comprehension

Story Summary: The fifth grade conducts a survey about sports. One group uses fractions to compile the results gathered, while another group uses decimals to compile results. To resolve the confusion, they switch and compile the information again.

Vocabulary: fraction, numerator, denominator, decimal, tenths, hundredths, thousandths

Responding Answers:
1. Write 0.8 as the fraction 8/10 and then simplify it by dividing the numerator and denominator by 2 to get 4/5. **2.** Change 2/5 to the equivalent fraction 4/10 and write 0.4. **3.** Change 1/4 to the equivalent fraction 25/100 and write 0.25. **4.** 0.5 is greatest; 1/50 is least. **Activity** 3/4, 1/5, 1/2, 3/5

Beautiful Geometry
by Marilyn Eden

Focus: polygons and help support student comprehension

Story Summary: *Beautiful Geometry* describes how triangles and quadrilaterals are used in several famous paintings and sculptures.

Vocabulary: triangle, quadrilateral, square, cube, rectangle, geometry, geometric shape, polygon

Responding Answers:
1. diamond 2. rectangle 3. triangle
Activity Students collect data and find the range, median, mode, and mean of the data.

Catching the Wind
by S. Ada Shevitz

Focus: area and help support student comprehension

Story Summary: *Catching the Wind* discusses the square sails and triangular sails used in the past on sailing ships and used today on sailboats. Students find the area of individual sails and the total area of all the sails on a boat.

Vocabulary: square, triangle, rectangle, trapezoid, area, base, height

Responding Answers:
1. rectangle, trapezoid, triangle **2.** 112.5 sq ft **3.** 169 sq ft
Activity Students design a sailboat with at least 2 sails and find the area of the sails.

Cranking Out the Numbers
by H. J. Serden, illustrated by Amanda Harvey

Focus: multiplying fractions

Story Summary: In *Cranking Out the Numbers*, Mr. Foster's fifth-grade class is planning to make ice cream. They need to triple the recipe to make enough, which means multiplying each fraction or mixed number by 3.

Vocabulary: fraction, numerator, denominator, multiply, mixed number, improper fraction

Responding Answers:
1. multiply it by 3 **2.** 7 cups **3.** 5 1/3 cups
Activity Students use fraction bar drawings or overhead fraction tiles to make up and solve problems using mixed numbers and fractions.

Damage Along a Fault Line
by M. L. Cuffney

Focus: mean, median, and mode and help support student comprehension

Story Summary: Earthquakes are the topic of *Damage Along a Fault Line*. Students study data on recent earthquakes. Then they learn to find the range of data and the mean, median, and mode of the earthquake data.

Vocabulary: range, line plot, mean, median, mode

Responding Answers:
1. 17 **2.** 11 **3.** 11 **4.** 132 ÷ 11 = 12
Activity Students collect data and find the range, median, mode, and mean of the data.

Data on the Endangered
by Dan Gulbis

Focus: interpreting data

Story Summary: Data on endangered animals is used to help students understand how to read and interpret data in charts, graphs, and text.

Vocabulary: compare, data, picture graph, chart, bar graph

Responding Answers:
1. The population has increased. **2.** reptiles **3.** 6 species
Activity The bar or picture graph should be organized to accurately reflect the number of classmates polled, all the endangered animal choices, and the results in uniform units.

Dewey and His Decimals
by Kathleen Cannon, illustrated by Stacey Schuett

Focus: decimal numbers and help support student comprehension

Story Summary: In *Dewey and His Decimals*, two student librarians are learning the Dewey Decimal system used to order books in the library.

Vocabulary: order, compare, decimal, hundredths, thousandths

Responding Answers:
1. 164, 261, 426, 641, 645 **2.** seven hundred eight and fifty-seven hundredths; 411.008
3. The greatest is 966.99; the least is 966.009. **4.** zero in hundredths place: 187.008 and 620.909; 8 in the thousandths place: 187.008 and 300.068
Activity Five out of six belong on the chart: 166.47 and 410.4: tenths place; 035.849 and 724.043: hundredths place; 537.834: thousandths place

Doubling Every Day
by Ben Williamson, illustrated by Lindy Burnett

Focus: multiplying decimals

Story Summary: In *Doubling Every Day*, Miguel gives his brother Marco a challenging math problem—to figure how much someone would get paid in 30 days if the salary started at $0.01 and doubled every day.

Vocabulary: estimate, multiply, decimal number, decimal point, factor

Responding Answers:
1. An estimate is a thoughtful guess about something. **2.** 70 × 30 = 2,100 **3.** A number with one or more digits to the right of a decimal point. **4.** The decimal point goes between the 6 and the 4, so the answer is 16.42.
Activity Check students' table answers.

Fossil Hunters
by Celie Petersvier

Focus: adding and subtracting fractions and help support student comprehension

Story Summary: Facts related to fossils are used to add and subtract fractions. Facts include the fraction of bones found in the most complete *T. rex* skeletons, and the fractions of living things that have hard parts that can become fossils.

Vocabulary: fraction, simplest form

Responding Answers:
1. 7/8 **2.** 5/12 **3.** 17/24
Activity Students use fraction bar drawings or fraction tiles to practice adding and subtracting fractions.

Fractions Add Up!
by J. Quinn Freeman, illustrated by Leslie Evans

Focus: fractions and mixed numbers

Story Summary: In *Fractions Add Up!*, the Dai family uses a map of the trails in a state park to plan a hike that is a good distance for everyone. They add the distances, which are fractions and mixed numbers, to find the total.

Vocabulary: fraction, sum, mixed number, improper fraction, simplest form

Responding Answers:
1. 2 1/3 **2.** 7/6 or 14/12 **3.** 1 1/6 **4.** Find the lowest common denominator, 6. Then use the lowest common denominator to find equivalent fractions. 1/3 = 2/6, and 1/2 = 3/6. Add 5/6 + 2/6 + 2/6 + 3/6 = 12/6. Write the sum in simplest form: 12/6 = 2.
Activity Students draw a walking path in a park that includes three of the distances listed. Then they add the distances.

Goldbach's Gift to Math
by Grant Peyton

Focus: prime and composite numbers

Story Summary: *Goldbach's Gift to Math* is a short biography of Christian Goldbach, a Russian mathematician who made many contributions to mathematics including his conjecture regarding prime numbers.

Vocabulary: factor, common factors, conjecture, prime number, composite number

Responding Answers:
1. Common factors are numbers that are factors of two or more numbers. The number 4 is a common factor of 12 and 16. **2.** 7 is a prime number. **3.** 2 and 20 and 4 and 10 are factor pairs for the number 40. **4.** 36 **5.** 2 or 3
Activity Equations will vary, but all equations should include two prime numbers with a sum that is an even number.

Graphing Practice
by Spencer Warren, illustrated by Nicole Tadgell

Focus: function tables and graphs

Story Summary: In *Graphing Practice*, Ella and Carlota are preparing for the softball team tryouts. Ella is discouraged until Carlota makes a plan for their practice sessions. She uses a function table and a coordinate grid to help them reach their goal.

Vocabulary: function table, coordinate grid, *x*-axis, *y*-axis, ordered pair, graph

Responding Answers:
1. 12 laps 2. (10, 30) 3. Sample answer: I don't know how many pitches Carlota made or how many times Ella missed the ball.
Activity Students make a function table and place the ordered pairs from their table on a coordinate grid.

Is This a Career for You?
by Donald Brach

Focus: coordinate grids

Story Summary: Students are introduced to careers that require reading a coordinate grid such as those of a helicopter rescue pilot, a sea pilot, and a paleontologist.

Vocabulary: coordinate grid, coordinate, point, ordered pair, origin, horizontal axis, vertical axis

Responding Answers:
1. two 2. (0, 0) 3. The first number tells you how many units to move along the horizontal axis. 4. 5 units
Activity Students mark equal units on grid axes and name them with letters or numbers. Answers are stated as ordered pairs, with the horizontal axis reading first.

Niagara Falls Numbers
by S. Ada Sheritz

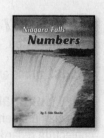

Focus: division

Story Summary: Numbers related to Niagara Falls are used in two-digit division problems. Facts about Niagara Falls include how many gallons of water go over the falls each minute and how many gallons are diverted to produce electricity.

Vocabulary: divide, estimate

Responding Answers:
1. 200,000 ÷ 5,000 = 40 miles 2. 4,812,000 ÷ 60 = 80,200 cubic feet per second
3. $1,548 ÷ 12 = $129 per night
Activity Students make a function table and place the ordered pairs from their table on a coordinate grid.

Seeking the Lowest Price
by Carter W. Ryan, illustrated by Kathleen Kemly

Focus: dividing decimals and help support student comprehension

Story Summary: In *Seeking the Lowest Price*, Janna is having trouble with her math lesson on dividing decimals until her mother relates dividing decimals to money and finding the lowest price per unit for an item.

Vocabulary: divide, decimal, decimal point, quotient, dividend

Responding Answers:
1. 4-lb: $0.61; 10-lb: $0.56 **2.** 12-lb: $0.50; 15-lb: $0.40 **3.** $0.05
Activity Sample answer: bottled water: 24-pack for $5.99; unit price: $0.25 per bottle.

Working on the Railroad
by H. J. Laager

Focus: addition and subtraction equations

Story Summary: Information on the building of the transcontinental railroad is used to help students practice solving addition and subtraction equations.

Vocabulary: total, how much more

Responding Answers:
1. 100 square miles **2.** $32,000 more **3.** 16 feet in 8 days; 28 feet in 2 weeks
4. 72 hours
Activity 10 miles - 200 miles of land
50 miles - 1,000 miles of land
100 miles - 2,000 miles of land

Name _____ Date _____

Two-Column Chart

Name _____ Date _____

Three-Column Chart

Name _____ Date _____

Four-Column Chart

Name _____ Date _____

Five-Column Chart

Name _____ Date _____

Six-Column Chart

Word Form Cards

Name _____ Date _____

Directions: Cut each card along the dotted line. Shuffle and put face-down in a pile.

one million, two hundred sixty-three thousand, four hundred nine	five hundred three thousand, two hundred forty-six	seventeen million, four hundred eighty-three thousand, two hundred six	two thousand, forty-eight
seven hundred two thousand, three hundred sixty-nine	four hundred three million, five hundred sixty-eight thousand, one hundred fifty-seven	six hundred three	two million, six hundred ninety-five thousand, seven hundred four
three hundred twelve million, four hundred sixty-five thousand, seven hundred eight	fifty thousand, four hundred sixty-eight	sixty-two million, seven hundred four thousand, three hundred nineteen	six thousand, one hundred twenty-three
nine hundred eighty-seven million, four hundred fifty-six thousand, three hundred one	three hundred fifteen thousand, two hundred ten	thirty-seven thousand, fifteen	two hundred seven thousand, three hundred sixty-nine

MathO Cards

		FREE		

		FREE		

Name _____   Date _____

Object List Worksheet

Directions: Write the abbreviation for the metric unit you would use to measure each object.

1. mass of a small rock _____

2. teacher's height _____

3. length of a crayon _____

4. distance from school to home _____

5. height of a telephone pole _____

6. amount of water in a water bottle _____

7. amount of water in a bathtub _____

8. mass of sand in a bucket _____

9. dose of medicine _____

10. length of a blade of grass _____

11. mass of a cell phone _____

12. mass of a beetle _____

13. length of a small snake _____

14. perimeter of a large rug _____

15. amount of milk in a glass _____

16. length of a large parking lot _____

17. height of a basketball player _____

18. distance a baseball is thrown _____

19. amount of paint in a can _____

20. length of an eraser _____

21. mass of a bag of potatoes _____

22. length of a full roll of ribbon _____

23. mass of a sugar cube _____

24. distance around a running track _____

25. mass of a piece of paper _____

26. length of an ant _____

27. amount of water in a raindrop _____

28. mass of a popcorn kernel _____

29. width of a piece of pencil lead _____

30. distance around your wrist _____

31. mass of a book _____

32. length of a hallway _____

33. perimeter of a sheet of notebook paper _____

34. mass of a toy truck _____

35. mass of a kitten _____

36. perimeter of the floor _____

37. amount of liquid in a spoon _____

38. height of a skyscraper _____

39. height of a cat _____

40. perimeter of a park _____

Object Card 1

Directions: Cut each card along the dotted line. Shuffle and put face-down in a pile.

5. height of a telephone pole	**10.** length of a blade of grass	**15.** amount of milk in a glass	**20.** length of an eraser
4. distance from school to home	**9.** dose of medicine	**14.** perimeter of a rug	**19.** amount of paint in a can
3. length of a crayon	**8.** mass of sand in a bucket	**13.** length of a small snake	**18.** distance a baseball is thrown
2. teacher's height	**7.** amount of water in a bathtub	**12.** mass of a beetle	**17.** height of a basketball player
1. mass of a small rock	**6.** amount of water in a water bottle	**11.** mass of a cell phone	**16.** length of a parking lot

Object Card 2

Directions: Cut each card along the dotted line. Shuffle and put face-down in a pile.

25. mass of a piece of paper	30. distance around your wrist	35. mass of a kitten	40. perimeter of a park
24. distance around a running track	29. width of a piece of pencil lead	34. mass of a toy truck	39. height of a cat
23. mass of a sugar cube	28. mass of a popcorn kernel	33. perimeter of a sheet of notebook paper	38. height of a skyscraper
22. length of a full roll of ribbon	27. amount of water in a raindrop	32. length of a hallway	37. amount of liquid in a spoon
21. mass of a bag of potatoes	26. length of an ant	31. mass of a book	36. perimeter of the floor

Name _____ Date _____

Circle/Spinner

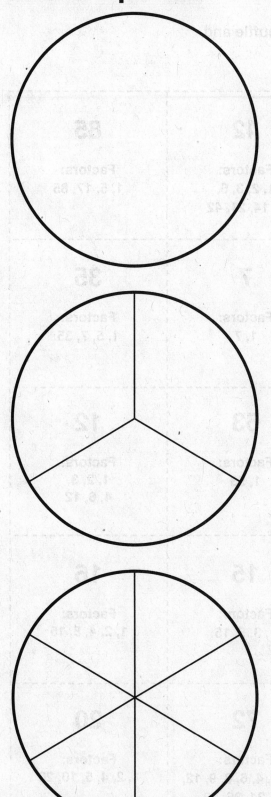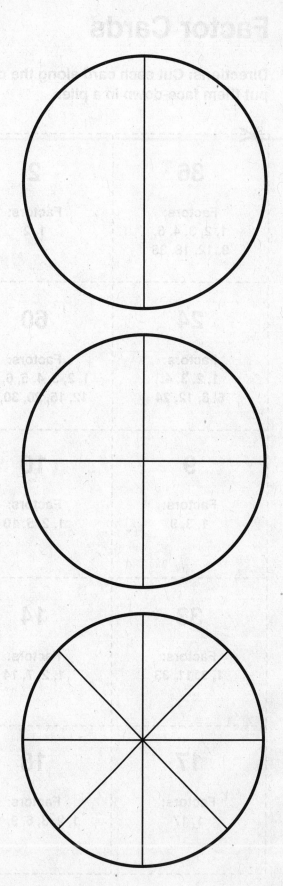

Factor Cards

Directions: Cut each card along the dotted line. Shuffle and put them face-down in a pile.

✂--

36 Factors: 1, 2, 3, 4, 6, 9, 12, 18, 36	**2** Factors: 1, 2	**42** Factors: 1, 2, 3, 6, 7, 14, 21, 42	**85** Factors: 1, 5, 17, 85
24 Factors: 1, 2, 3, 4, 6, 8, 12, 24	**60** Factors: 1, 2, 3, 4, 5, 6, 10, 12, 15, 20, 30, 60	**7** Factors: 1, 7	**35** Factors: 1, 5, 7, 35
9 Factors: 1, 3, 9	**10** Factors: 1, 2, 5, 10	**53** Factors: 1, 53	**12** Factors: 1, 2, 3, 4, 6, 12
33 Factors: 1, 3, 11, 33	**14** Factors: 1, 2, 7, 14	**15** Factors: 1, 3, 5, 15	**16** Factors: 1, 2, 4, 8, 16
17 Factors: 1, 17	**18** Factors: 1, 2, 3, 6, 9, 18	**72** Factors: 1, 2, 3, 4, 6, 8, 9, 12, 18, 24, 36, 72	**20** Factors: 1, 2, 4, 5, 10, 20

Name _____   Date _____

Figure Cards

Directions: Cut each card along the dotted line. Shuffle and put them face-down in a pile.

1.	2.	3.	4.
5.	6.	7.	8.
9.	10.	11.	12.
13.	14.	15.	16.
17.	18.	19.	20.

Name _____ Date _____

Decimal Cards

Directions: Cut each card along the dotted line. Shuffle and put face-down in a pile.

1.87	1.02	1.25	1.10
1.30	1.35	0.15	0.37
0.95	0.58	0.25	0.85
0.67	0.35	0.05	0.52
1.75	0.65	1.62	1.40

Name _____ Date _____

Money Cards 1

Directions: Cut each card along the dotted line.

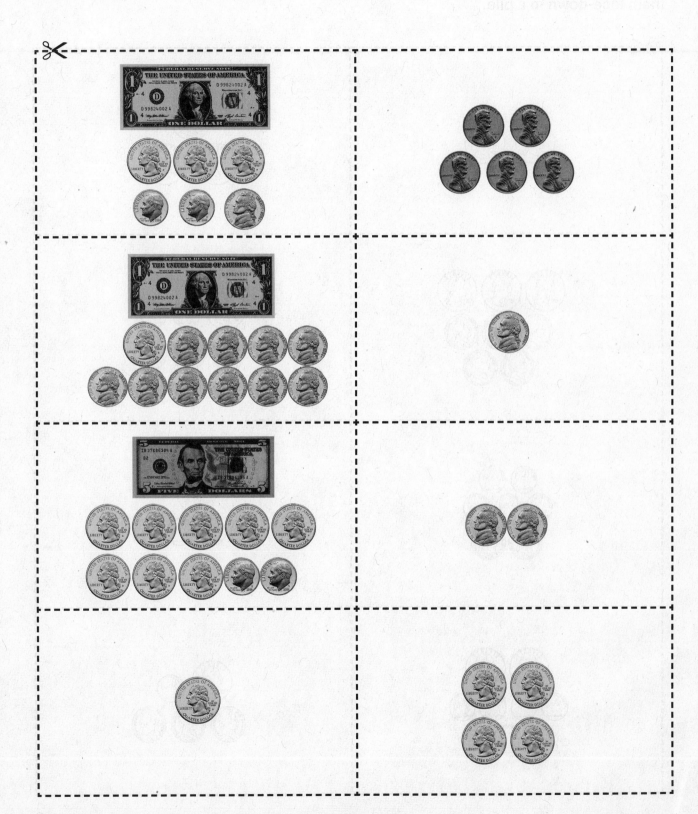

Money Cards 2

Directions: Cut each card along the dotted line. Shuffle and put them face-down in a pile.

Name _____   Date _____

Bingo Playing Cards

Directions: Cut each card along the dotted line. Shuffle and put them face-down in a pile.

$\dfrac{1}{4}$	$\dfrac{1}{25}$	$\dfrac{4}{5}$	$\dfrac{2}{25}$
$\dfrac{3}{25}$	$\dfrac{1}{1}$	$\dfrac{5}{8}$	$\dfrac{4}{25}$
$\dfrac{1}{2}$	$\dfrac{2}{5}$	$\dfrac{12}{25}$	$\dfrac{7}{8}$
$\dfrac{1}{5}$	$\dfrac{16}{25}$	$\dfrac{3}{4}$	$\dfrac{3}{8}$
$\dfrac{1}{8}$	$\dfrac{7}{25}$	$\dfrac{7}{10}$	$\dfrac{3}{10}$
$\dfrac{1}{10}$	$\dfrac{3}{5}$	$\dfrac{9}{10}$	$\dfrac{21}{25}$

Name _____ Date _____

Bingo Game Cards

Directions: Cut each card along the dotted line.

B	I	N	G	O
0.04	0.75	0.25	0.28	0.5
0.875	0.64	0.9	0.625	0.2
0.6	0.8	Free	0.12	1
0.16	0.7	0.1	0.125	0.08
0.375	0.48	0.3	0.4	0.84

B	I	N	G	O
0.9	0.875	0.625	0.64	0.2
0.84	0.6	0.12	0.8	1
0.1	0.16	Free	0.7	0.08
0.25	0.04	0.28	0.75	0.5
0.3	0.375	0.4	0.48	0.125

3 × 3 Grid

Decimal Pair Cards

Directions: Cut each card along the dotted line. Shuffle and put them face-down in a pile.

0.07, 0.7	**0.4, 0.44**	**42.36, 5.7**
0.67, 0.2	**0.8, 0.9**	**27.4, 0.86**
0.9, 0.06	**0.08, 0.09**	**7.23, 4.08**
0.25, 0.25	**8.23, 51.6**	**22.54, 18.93**
0.35, 0.53	**0.13, 0.01**	**74.82, 6.1**

Simplified Fractions Board/Cards

Directions: To use as cards, cut along the dotted line. Shuffle and put them face-down in a pile.

$\dfrac{1}{5}$	$\dfrac{3}{5}$	$\dfrac{7}{8}$	$\dfrac{5}{6}$
$\dfrac{2}{9}$	$\dfrac{1}{6}$	$\dfrac{2}{3}$	$\dfrac{5}{7}$
$\dfrac{3}{4}$	$\dfrac{1}{2}$	$\dfrac{7}{10}$	$\dfrac{4}{9}$
$\dfrac{1}{3}$	$\dfrac{3}{10}$	$\dfrac{2}{5}$	$\dfrac{1}{4}$

Name _____ Date _____

Mixed Fraction Board

Name _____ Date _____

Centimeter Grid

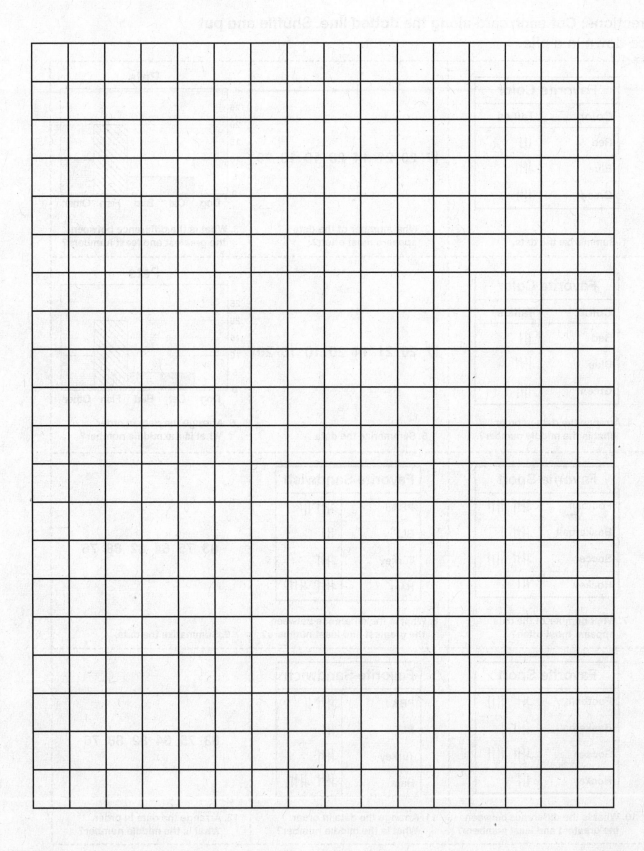

Name _____ Date _____

Data Deck Cards

Directions: Cut each card along the dotted line. Shuffle and put face-down in a pile.

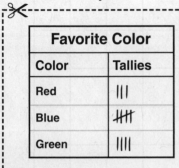

Favorite Color	
Color	**Tallies**
Red	|||
Blue	＃＃
Green	||||

1. Summarize the data.

17 20 21 14 20 10 10 20

2. What number of the data appears most often?

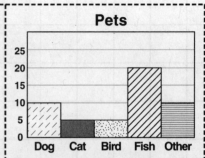

Pets

3. What is the difference between the greatest and least numbers?

Favorite Color	
Color	**Tallies**
Red	|||
Blue	＃＃
Green	||||

4. Arrange the data in order. What is the middle number?

17 20 21 14 20 10 10 20

5. Summarize the data.

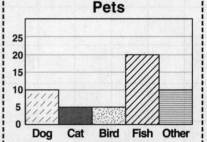

Pets

6. Arrange the data in order. What is the middle number?

Favorite Sport	
Football	＃＃ ||||
Basketball	＃＃	
Soccer	＃＃ ||||
Hockey	|||

7. What number of the data appears most often?

Favorite Sandwich	
PB&J	＃＃ ||
BLT	|||
Turkey	＃＃
Ham	＃＃ ＃＃

8. What is the difference between the greatest and least numbers?

83 75 64 82 88 76

9. Summarize the data.

Favorite Sport	
Football	＃＃ ||||
Basketball	＃＃	
Soccer	＃＃ ||||
Hockey	|||

10. What is the difference between the greatest and least numbers?

Favorite Sandwich	
PB&J	＃＃ ||
BLT	|||
Turkey	＃＃
Ham	＃＃ ＃＃

11. Arrange the data in order. What is the middle number?

83 75 64 82 88 76

12. Arrange the data in order. What is the middle number?

Name _____ Date _____

Satellite Gameboard 1

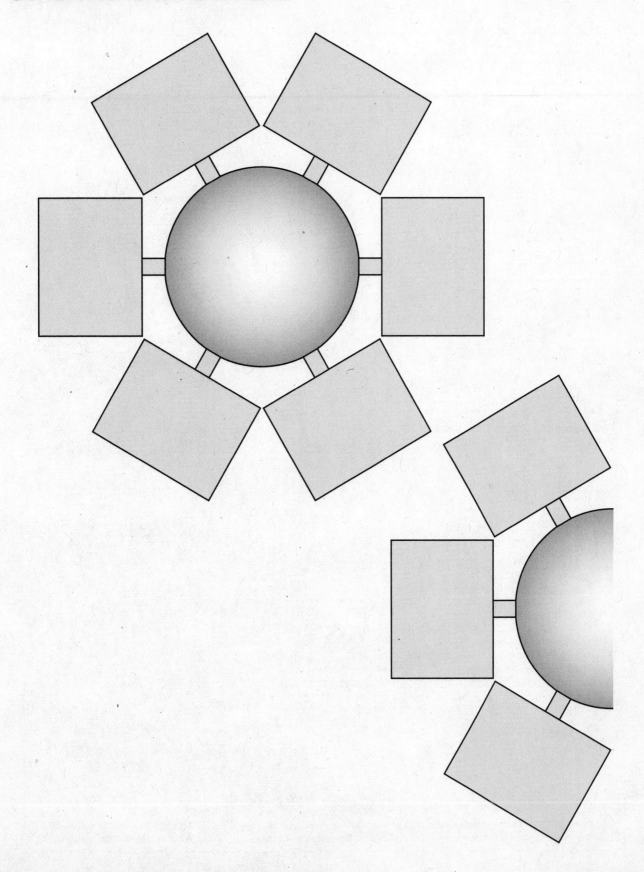

Name _____ Date _____

Satellite Gameboard 2

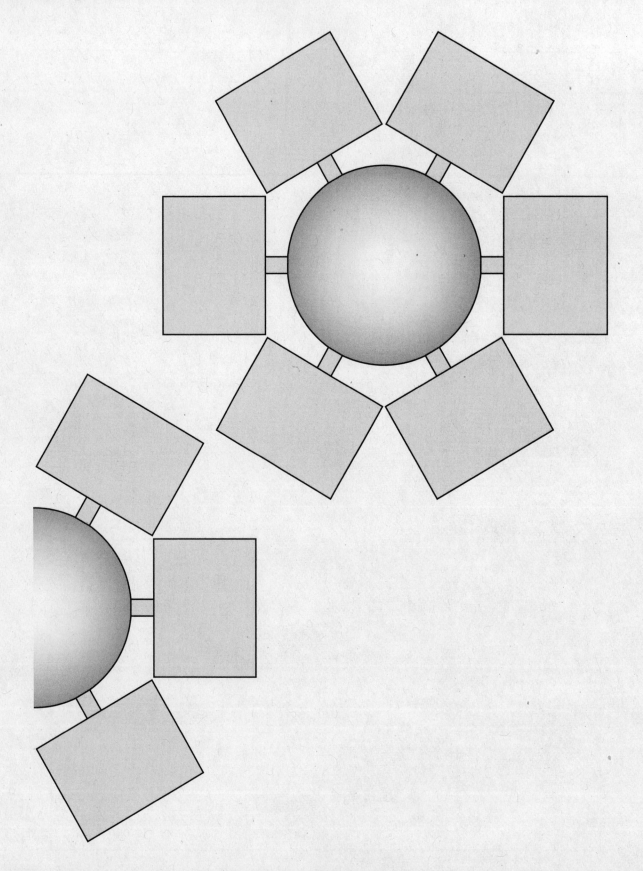

Pattern Block Equation Cards

Directions: Cut each card along the dotted line. Shuffle and put them face-up in a pile.

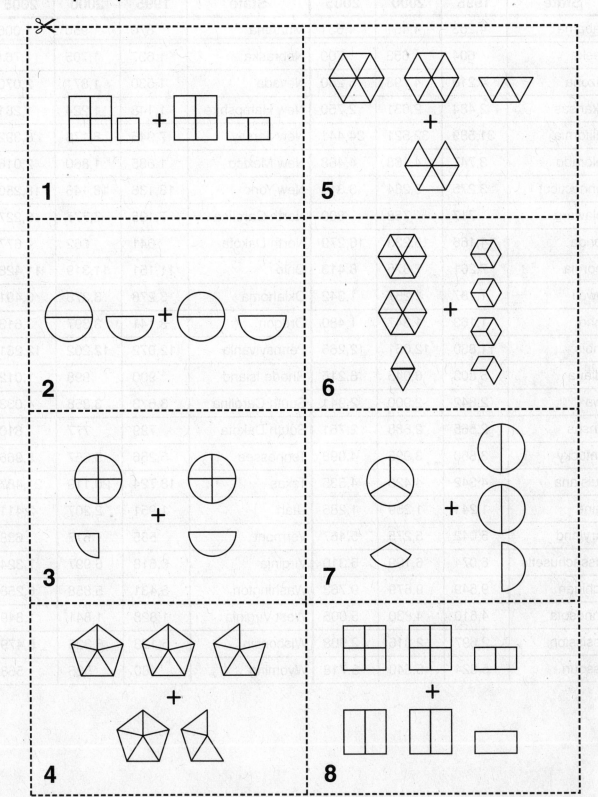

Name _____ Date _____

State Populations (in Thousands)

State	1995	2000	2005	State	1995	2000	2005
Alabama	4,253	4,451	4,631	Montana	870	950	1,006
Alaska	604	653	700	Nebraska	1,637	1,705	1,761
Arizona	4,218	4,798	5,230	Nevada	1,530	1,871	2,070
Arkansas	2,484	2,631	2,750	New Hampshire	1,148	1,224	1,281
California	31,589	32,521	34,441	New Jersey	7,945	8,178	8,392
Colorado	3,747	4,168	4,468	New Mexico	1,685	1,860	2,016
Connecticut	3,275	3,284	3,318	New York	18,136	18,146	18,250
Delaware	717	768	800	North Carolina	7,195	7,777	8,227
Florida	14,166	15,233	16,279	North Dakota	641	662	677
Georgia	7,201	7,875	8,413	Ohio	11,151	11,319	11,428
Hawaii	1,187	1,257	1,342	Oklahoma	3,278	3,373	3,491
Idaho	1,163	1,347	1,480	Oregon	3,141	3,397	3,613
Illinois	11,830	12,051	12,266	Pennsylvania	12,072	12,202	12,281
Indiana	5,803	6,045	6,215	Rhode Island	990	998	1,012
Iowa	2,842	2,900	2,941	South Carolina	3,673	3,858	4,033
Kansas	2,565	2,668	2,761	South Dakota	729	777	810
Kentucky	3,860	3,995	4,098	Tennessee	5,256	5,657	5,966
Louisiana	4,342	4,425	4,535	Texas	18,724	20,119	21,487
Maine	1,241	1,259	1,285	Utah	1,951	2,207	2,411
Maryland	5,042	5,275	5,467	Vermont	585	617	638
Massachusetts	6,074	6,199	6,310	Virginia	6,618	6,997	7,324
Michigan	9,549	9,679	9,763	Washington	5,431	5,858	6,258
Minnesota	4,610	4,830	5,005	West Virginia	1,828	1,841	1,849
Mississippi	2,697	2,816	2,908	Wisconsin	5,123	5,326	5,479
Missouri	5,324	5,540	5,718	Wyoming	480	525	568

Name _____ Date _____

State Capital Temperatures (degrees Fahrenheit)

City, State	Jan.	Feb.	March	April	May	June	July	Aug.	Sept.	Oct.	Nov.	Dec.
Sacramento, California	46	51	54	59	65	71	76	75	72	64	53	46
Austin, Texas	50	54	61	69	75	82	85	85	80	70	60	53
Albany, New York	22	24	34	47	58	67	72	70	61	51	40	27
Tallahassee, Florida	52	55	61	67	74	80	82	81	78	69	60	54
Harrisburg, Pennsylvania	30	32	41	52	62	71	76	74	67	55	44	34
Springfield, Illinois	27	30	41	53	64	73	78	75	68	57	43	31
Columbus, Ohio	28	31	41	52	62	71	75	73	66	54	43	33
Lansing, Michigan	22	24	33	46	57	67	71	69	61	50	38	27
Trenton, New Jersey	31	33	42	52	62	71	76	75	67	56	47	36
Atlanta, Georgia	43	46	53	62	70	77	79	79	73	63	53	45
Raleigh, North Carolina	40	43	50	60	67	75	79	77	71	60	51	43
Richmond, Virginia	38	40	48	58	66	75	78	77	71	59	50	41
Olympia, Washington	38	41	44	48	54	59	63	63	59	50	43	39
Baton Rouge, Louisiana	51	54	61	68	75	81	82	82	78	69	59	53
Honolulu, Hawaii	73	73	74	75	77	79	80	81	81	80	77	74
Providence, Rhode Island	29	30	38	48	58	67	73	72	64	54	44	33
Helena, Montana	19	26	33	43	53	61	68	67	56	45	32	22
Juneau, Alaska	24	28	33	40	47	54	56	55	50	42	33	28
Montpelier, Vermont	17	19	27	41	52	62	67	64	56	47	35	21

Computation Recording Sheet

Name _____ Date _____

Two-Digit Times Two-Digit Multiplication Mat

Name _____ Date _____

Prism Nets

Directions: Cut each net along the solid line for each prism. Fold on the dotted line. Make sure the labels are on the outside and tape each figure to make a prism. Make sure you can open your prism at the top.

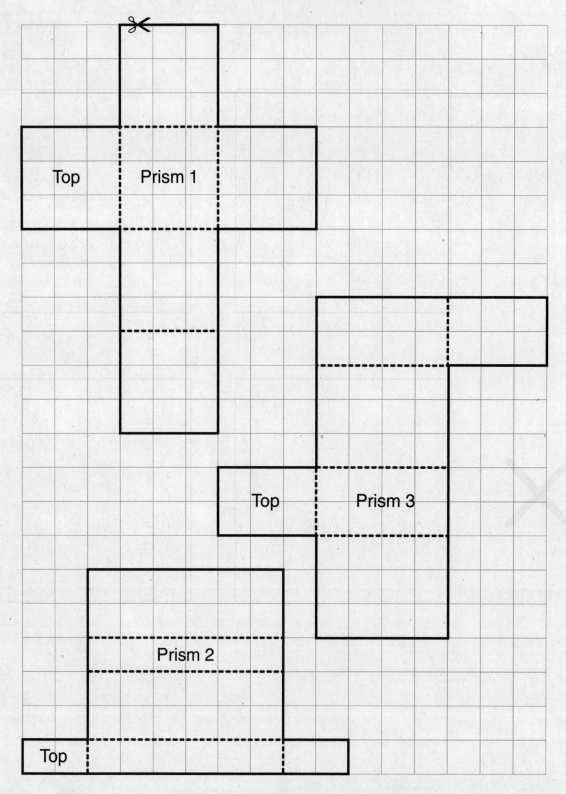

Number Cards

Directions: Cut each card along the dotted line. Shuffle and put them face-down in a pile.

0	1	2	3
4	5	6	7
8	9	10	11
12	13	14	15
16	17	18	19

Decimal Cards 3

Directions: Cut each card along the dotted line. Shuffle and put them face-up in rows.

1.72	2.3	4.8
4.06	16.4	9.88
20.9	40.6	0.1

Cube Net

Directions: Cut along the solid line. Fold on the dotted line. Glue or tape the flaps in place.

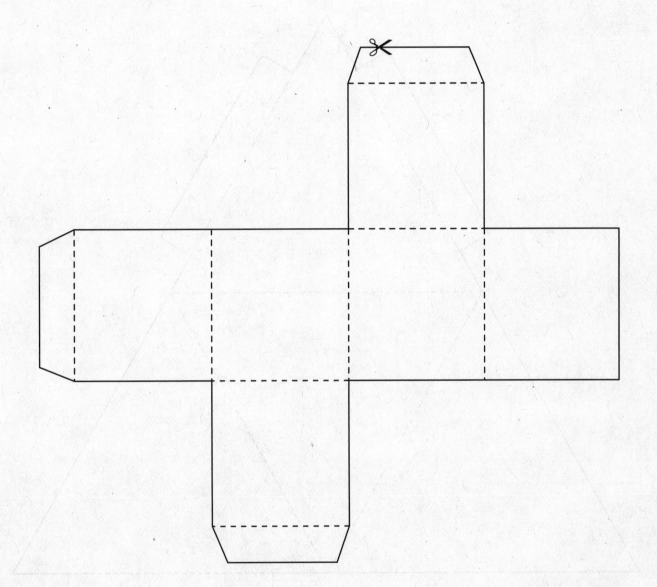

Triangular Pyramid Net

Directions: Cut along the solid line. Fold on the dotted line. Glue or tape the flaps in place.

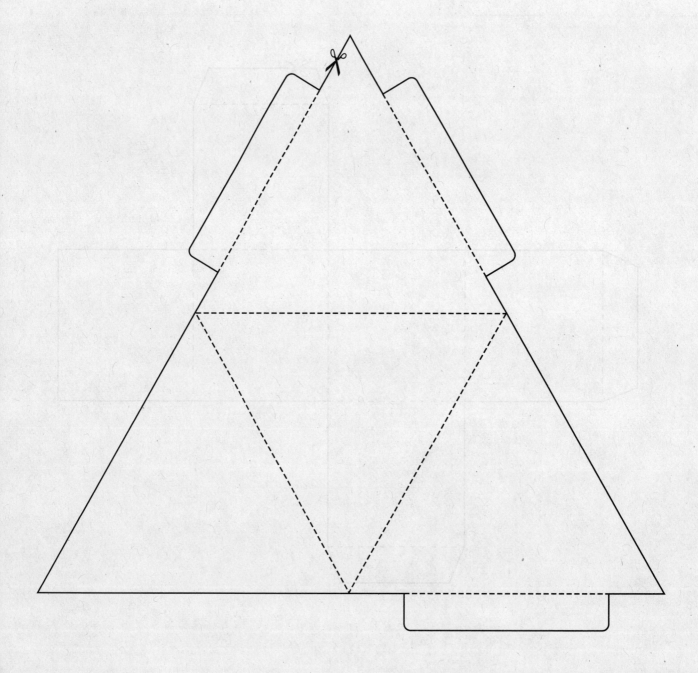

Square Pyramid Net

Directions: Cut along the solid line. Fold on the dotted line. Glue or tape the flaps in place.

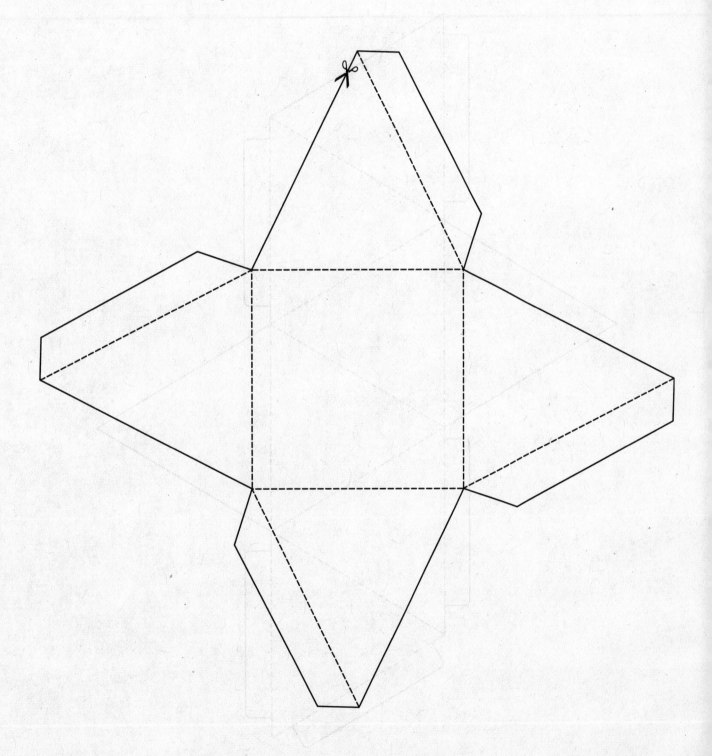

Octahedron Net

Directions: Cut along the solid line. Fold on the dotted line. Glue or tape the flaps in place.

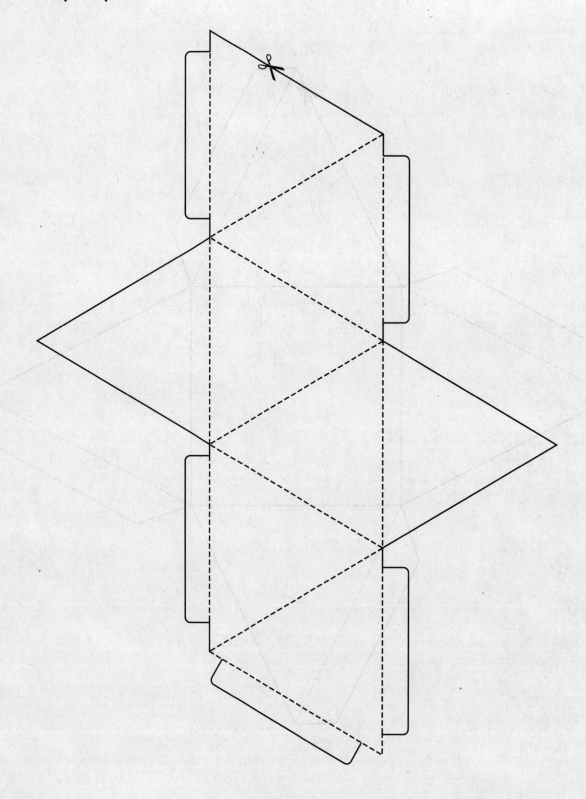

Name _____   Date _____

Dodecahedron Net

Directions: Cut along the solid line. Fold on the dotted line. Glue or tape the flaps in place.

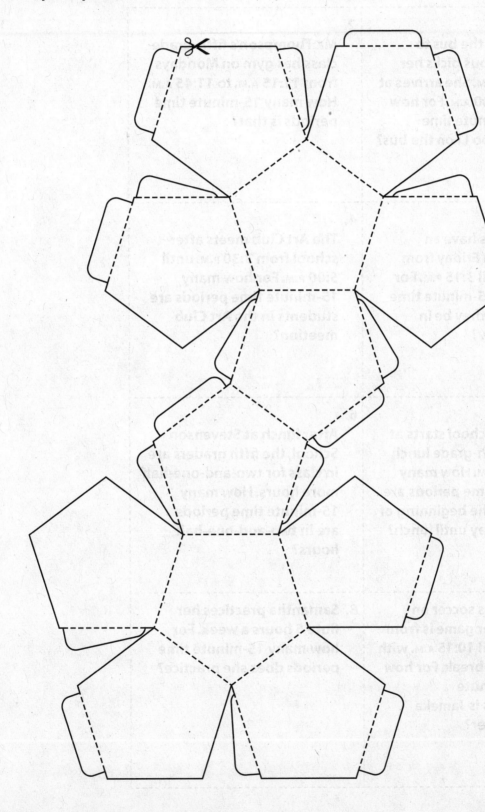

© Houghton Mifflin Harcourt Publishing Company

Name _____ Date _____

Division Story Cards

Directions: Cut each card along the dotted line. Shuffle and put face-down in a pile.

✂--

1.

Soo Li takes the bus to school. The bus picks her up at 7:45 A.M. She arrives at school at 8:30 A.M. For how many 15-minute time periods is Soo Li on the bus?

2.

Mr. Thompson's fifth-grade class has gym on Mondays from 11:15 A.M. to 11:45 A.M. How many 15-minute time periods is that?

3.

The students have an assembly on Friday from 2:00 P.M. until 3:15 P.M. For how many 15-minute time periods will they be in the assembly?

4.

The Art Club meets after school from 3:30 P.M. until 5:00 P.M. For how many 15-minute time periods are students in the Art Club meeting?

5.

Stevenson School starts at 8:45 A.M. Fifth-grade lunch is at 12:00 P.M. How many 15-minute time periods are there from the beginning of the school day until lunch?

6.

After lunch at Stevenson School, the fifth graders are in class for two-and-one-half more hours. How many 15-minute time periods are in two-and-one-half hours?

7. Jameka plays soccer on Saturday. Her game is from 9:00 A.M. until 10:15 A.M. with a 15-minute break. For how many 15-minute time periods is Jameka playing soccer?

8. Samantha practices her flute 5 hours a week. For how many 15-minute time periods does she practice?

Name _____ Date _____

Decide and Divide Table Worksheet

Directions: Use estimation to decide which numbers from column A and column B you can divide to get the highest quotient. Each number may be used only once.

A			B		
72	38	41	417	828	207
19	66	96	675	919	341
23	87	52	550	178	723
18	29	43	143	385	649
57	65	97	270	425	782
76	84	31	878	995	516

Name _____ Date _____

Geometric Picture Cards

Directions: Cut each card along the dotted line. Shuffle and put them face-down in a pile.

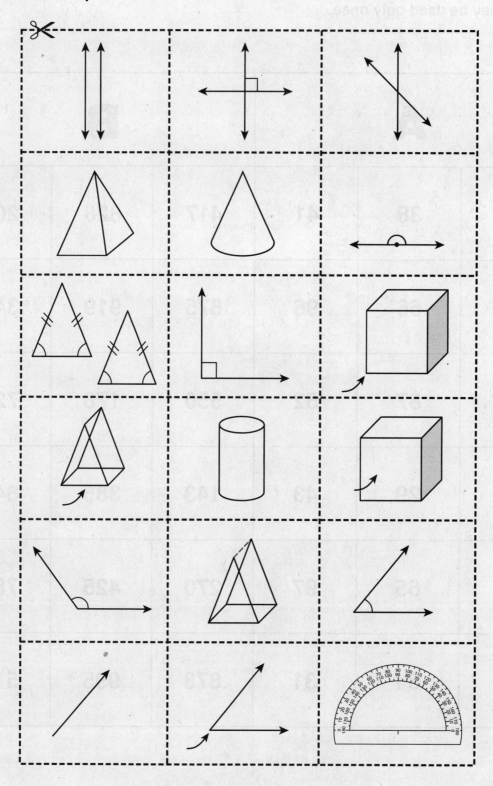

Hundredths Grids

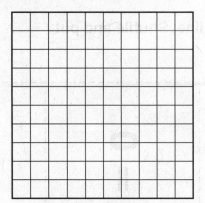
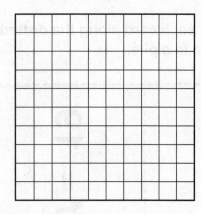
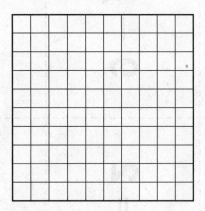
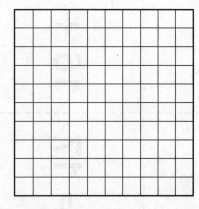
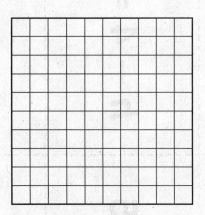
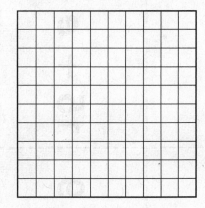
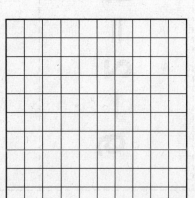
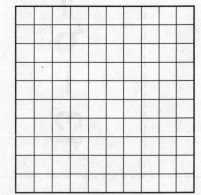

Equation Cards 1

Directions: Cut each card along the dotted line. Shuffle and put them face-down in a pile.

$14 - c = 8$	$16 + f = 19$	$9 - j = 0$	$m - 4 = 4$
$b + 9 = 16$	$15 + e = 17$	$h - 4 = 2$	$l - 2 = 2$
$a + 6 = 11$	$13 - d = 9$	$g - 2 = 5$	$k - 5 = 0$

Equation Cards 2

Directions: Cut each card along the dotted line. Shuffle and put them face-down in a pile.

$47 + q = 50$	$70 - t = 61$	$47 - w = 42$	$100 - z = 96$
$29 - p = 22$	$30 - s = 26$	$26 + v = 29$	$y + 92 = 188$
$6 - n = 4$	$79 + r = 80$	$u + 57 = 58$	$78 - x = 76$

3-D Gameboard 1

Directions: Attach to 3-D Gameboard 2.

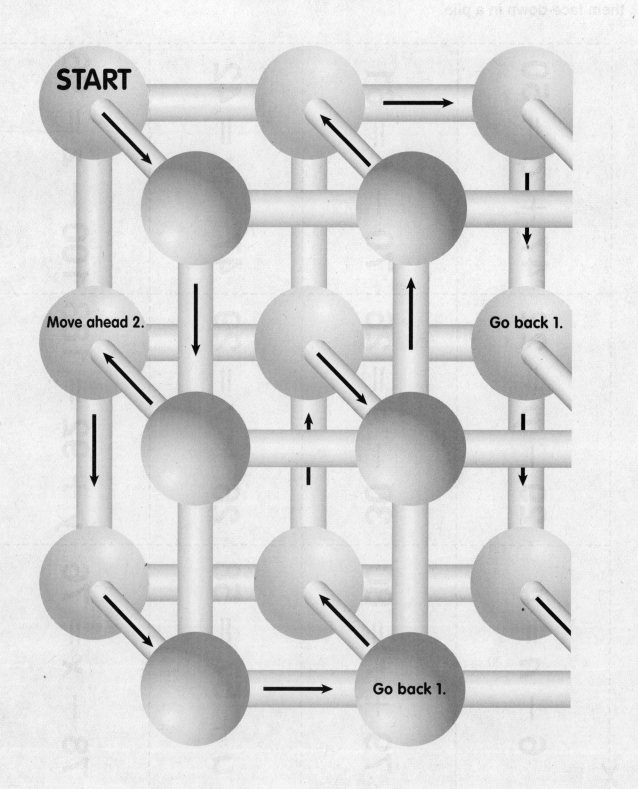

START

Move ahead 2.

Go back 1.

Go back 1.

3-D Gameboard 2

Directions: Attach to 3-D Gameboard 1.

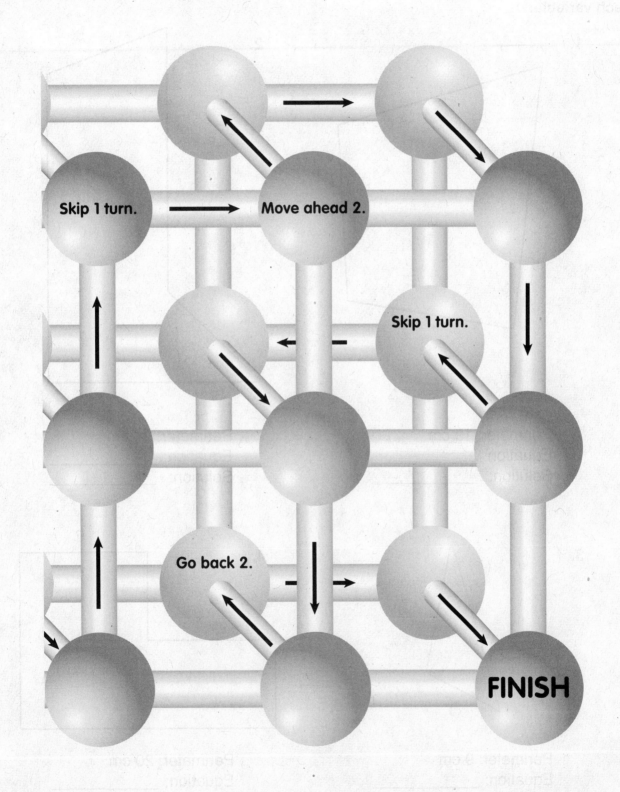

What's Missing? Worksheet

Directions: Write and solve an equation to find the value of each variable.

1.

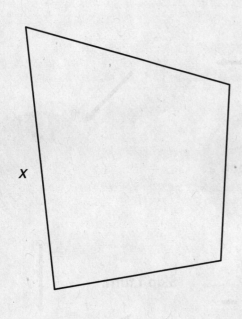

Perimeter: 19 cm

Equation: _____

Solution: _____

2.

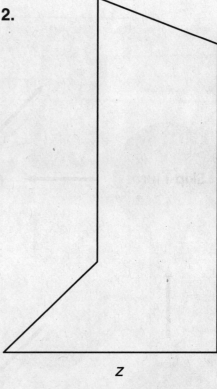

Perimeter: 24 cm

Equation: _____

Solution: _____

3.

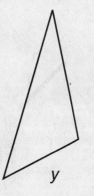

Perimeter: 9 cm

Equation: _____

Solution: _____

4.

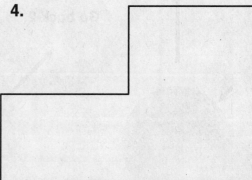

Perimeter: 20 cm

Equation: _____

Solution: _____

Coordinate Figure Worksheet

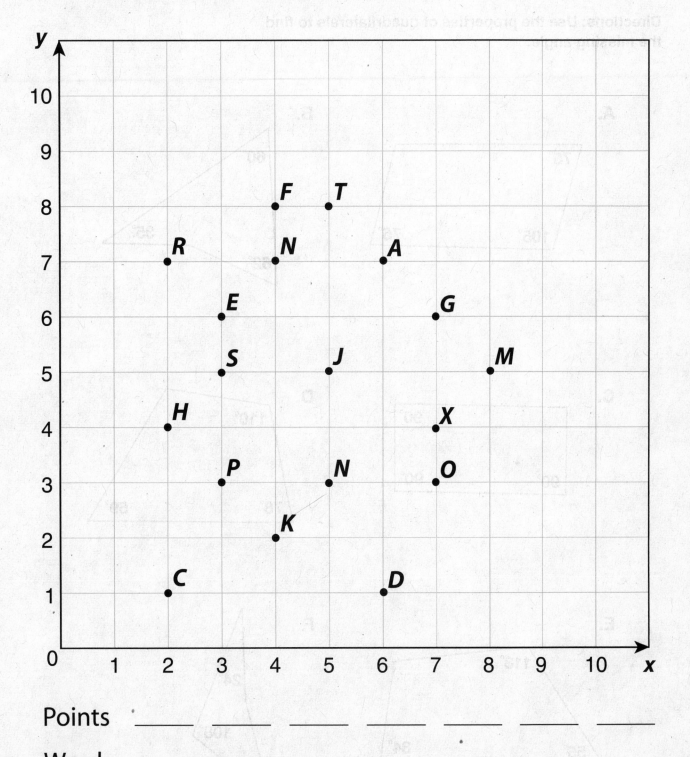

Points ____ ____ ____ ____ ____ ____

Word ____ ____ ____ ____ ____ ____

Quadrilaterals Worksheet

Directions: Use the properties of quadrilaterals to find the missing angle.

A.

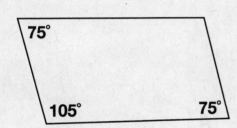

B.

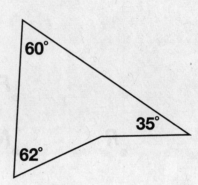

C.

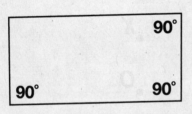

D.

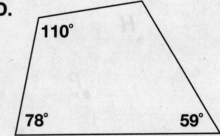

E.

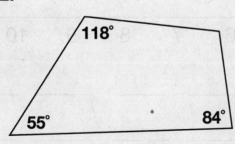

F.

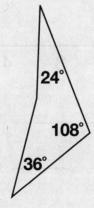

Name _____ Date _____

Triangles Worksheet

Directions: Use a protractor to measure the angles.

A.

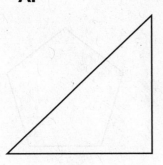

D.

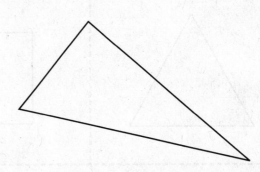

B.

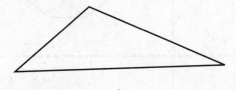

E.

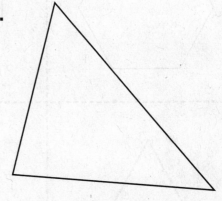

C.

F.

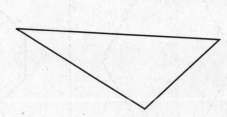

Polygon Puzzles Cards

Directions: Cut out the bottom two rows of polygons. Cut the remaining cards along the dotted line. Put them face-down in rows.

Prime or Composite?

Ready!

2 players

Set!

- 29 slips of paper
- Paper bag
- 30 counters
- 2 coins

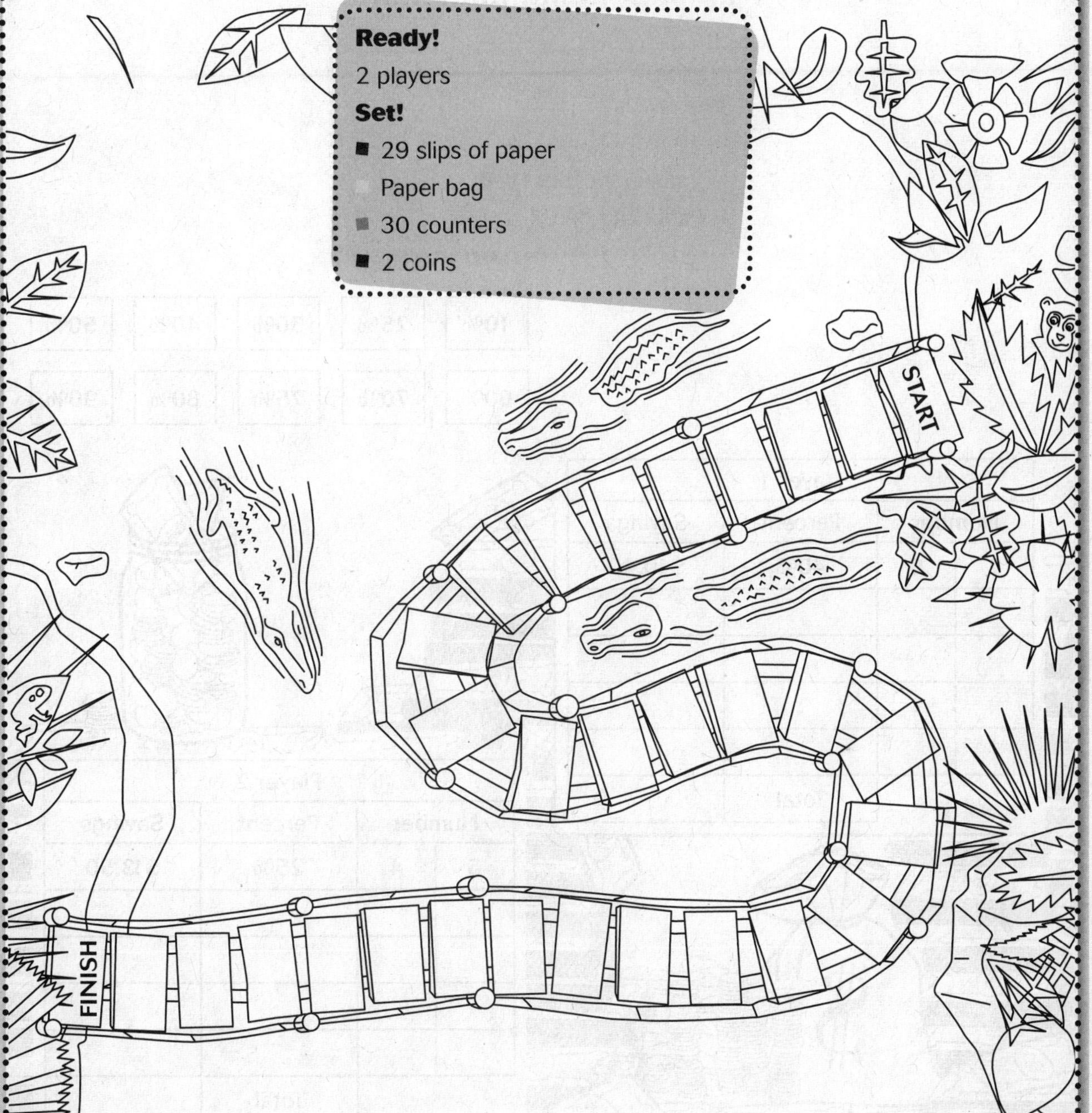

START

FINISH

Savings Account

Savers

2 players

Materials

- 10 index cards
- 2 number cubes (1–6)
- Paper and pencil

10%	25%	30%	40%	50%
60%	70%	75%	80%	90%

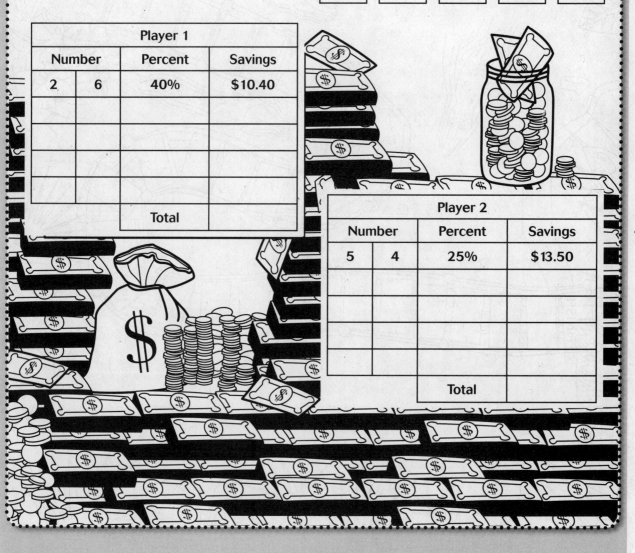

Player 1

Number		Percent	Savings
2	6	40%	$10.40
	Total		

Player 2

Number		Percent	Savings
5	4	25%	$13.50
	Total		

Ride the Course

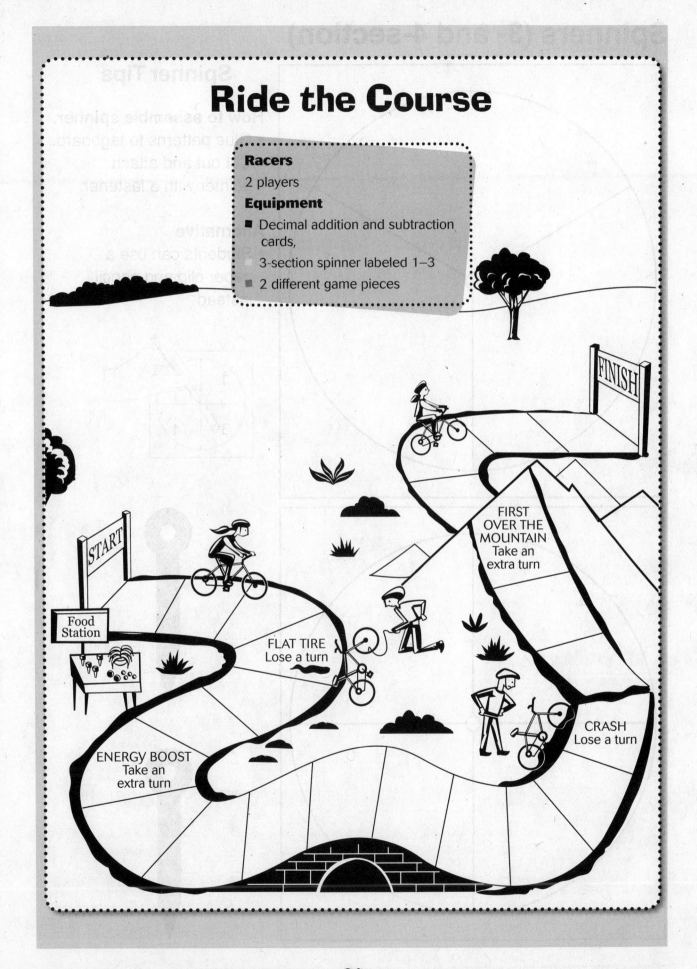

Racers

2 players

Equipment

- Decimal addition and subtraction cards,
- 3-section spinner labeled 1–3
- 2 different game pieces

FINISH

FIRST
OVER THE
MOUNTAIN
Take an
extra turn

START

Food
Station

FLAT TIRE
Lose a turn

CRASH
Lose a turn

ENERGY BOOST
Take an
extra turn

Spinners (3- and 4-section)

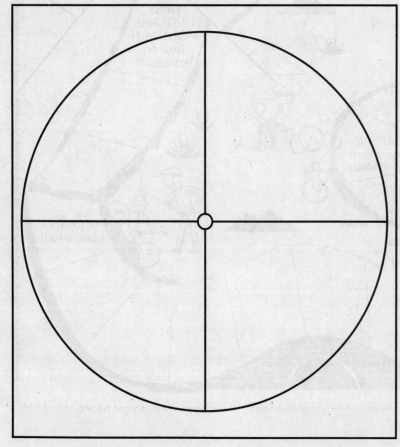

Spinner Tips

How to assemble spinner.
- Glue patterns to tagboard.
- Cut out and attach pointer with a fastener.

Alternative
- Students can use a paper clip and pencil instead.

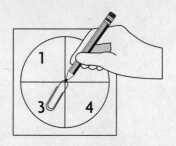

What's the Difference?

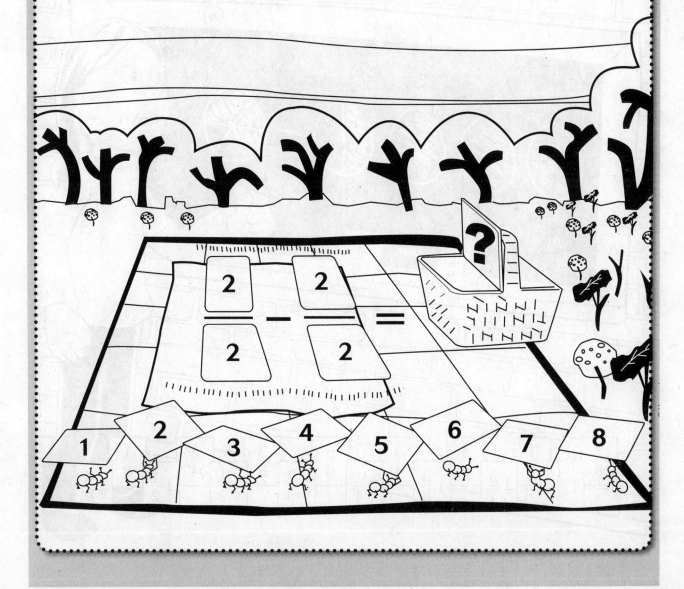

Picture Problems

Decimal Challenge

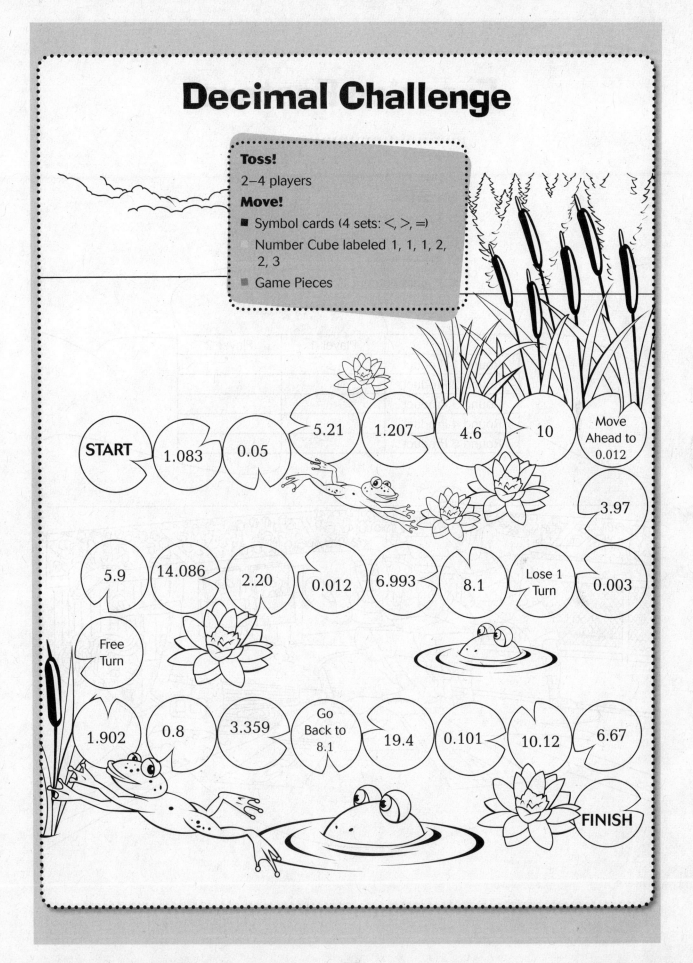

Toss!
2–4 players
Move!
- Symbol cards (4 sets: <, >, =)
- Number Cube labeled 1, 1, 1, 2, 2, 3
- Game Pieces

START 1.083 0.05 5.21 1.207 4.6 10 Move Ahead to 0.012

3.97

5.9 14.086 2.20 0.012 6.993 8.1 Lose 1 Turn 0.003

Free Turn

1.902 0.8 3.359 Go Back to 8.1 19.4 0.101 10.12 6.67

FINISH

Fraction Factors

Players

2 students

Materials

- Game boards
- 3 sets of number cards (1–9)
- Score chart
- Paper and pencils

	Player 1	Player 2
Round 1 Product		
Round 2 Product		
Round 3 Product		
Round 4 Product		
Round 5 Product		

Just Checking

It's a Toss-Up

GAME RESULTS

SCORE

ROUND

Game

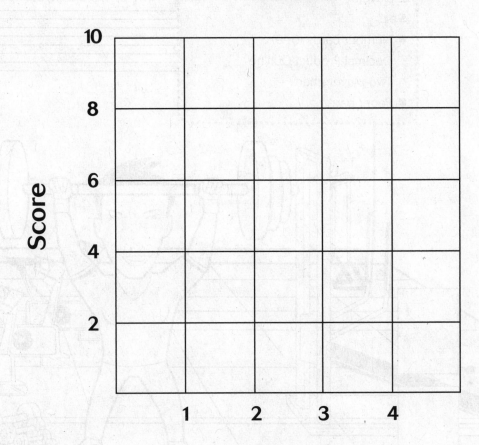

Score

10

8

6

4

2

1   2   3   4

Round

Powerful Products

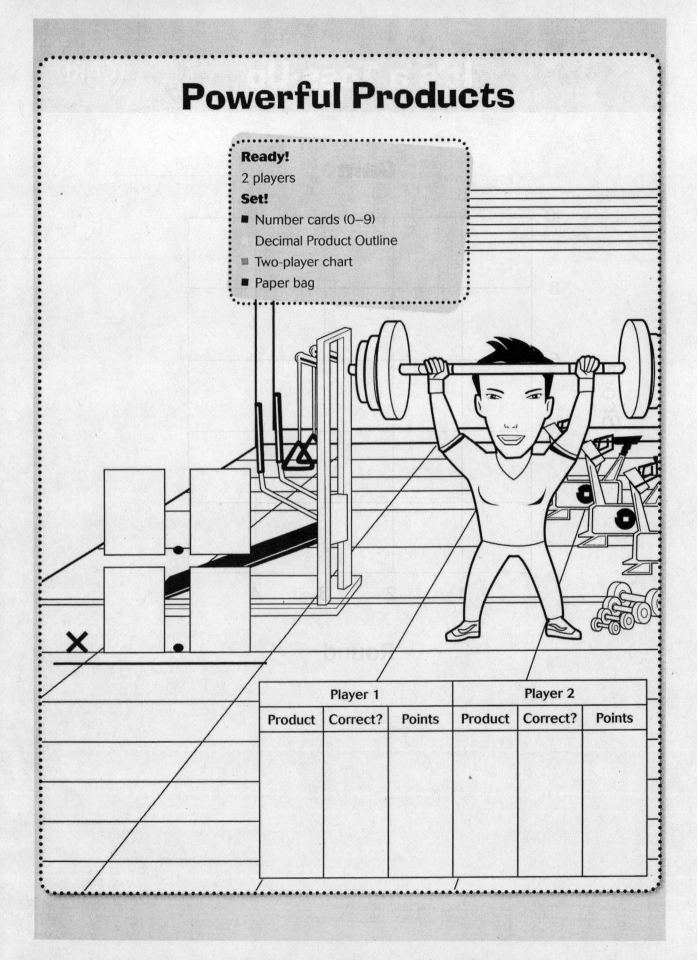

Ready!

2 players

Set!

- Number cards (0–9)
  Decimal Product Outline
- Two-player chart
- Paper bag

	Player 1			Player 2	
Product	Correct?	Points	Product	Correct?	Points

Predicting Sums

Players

4 players

Materials

■ 2 number cubes labeled 1–6

□ Tally table

Tally Table

2
3
4
5
6
7
8
9

3 + 6

6 + 3

4 + 5

5 + 4   9

5 + 5

4 + 6

10   6 + 4

6 + 5

11   5 + 6

1   5

Match Up

What's Your Angle?

	Player 1			Player 2		
	Estimate	Actual Measure	Difference	Estimate	Actual Measure	Difference
Round 1	75°	62°	13°			
Round 2						
Round 3						
Round 4						
Round 5						

© Houghton Mifflin Harcourt Publishing Company   **What's Your Angle?**

Around the Block

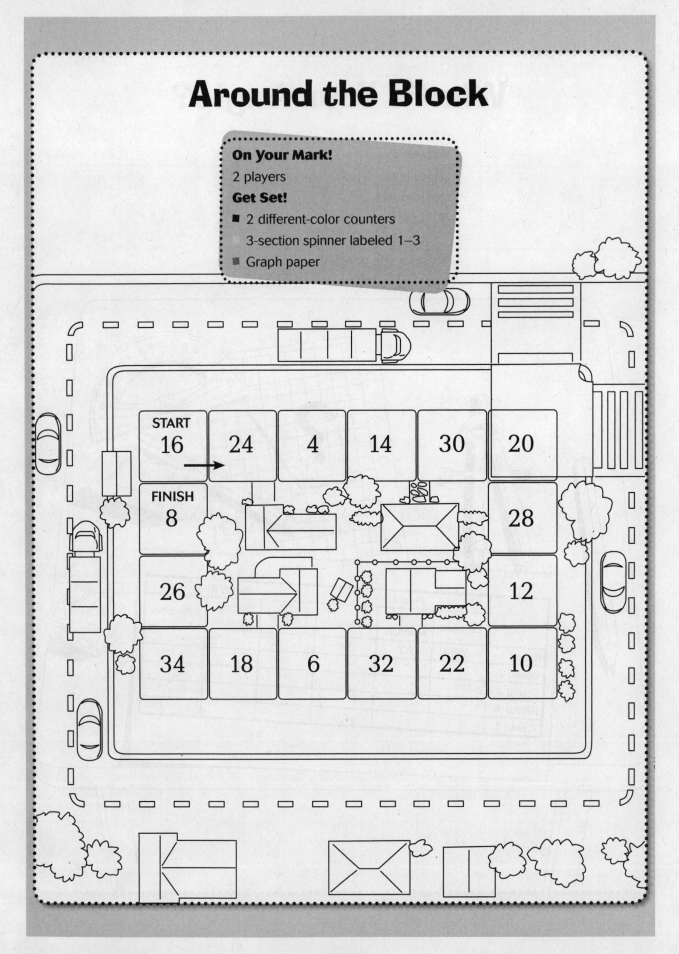

On Your Mark!

2 players

Get Set!

■ 2 different-color counters
○ 3-section spinner labeled 1–3
■ Graph paper

| START 16 | 24 | 4 | 14 | 30 | 20 |

| FINISH 8 | | | | | 28 |

| 26 | | | | | 12 |

| 34 | 18 | 6 | 32 | 22 | 10 |

Model Makers

Players

4 players

Materials

- Toothpicks
- 24 slips of paper
- Container

I am a quadrilateral with exactly one pair of parallel sides.

I am

I am

I am

I am

Triple Play

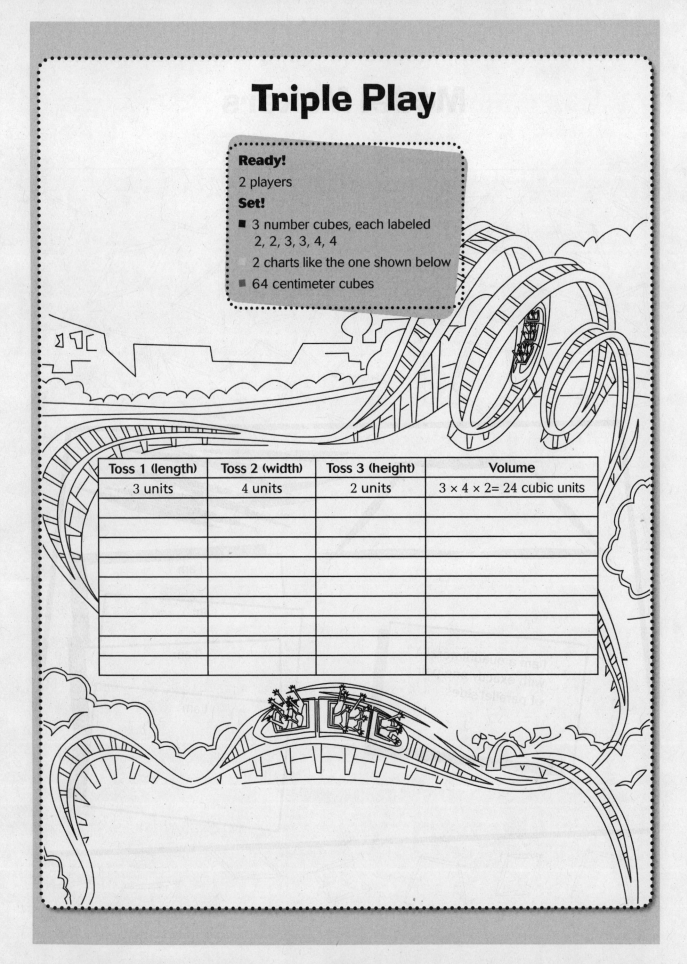

Ready!

2 players

Set!

- 3 number cubes, each labeled
  2, 2, 3, 3, 4, 4
- 2 charts like the one shown below
- 64 centimeter cubes

Toss 1 (length)	Toss 2 (width)	Toss 3 (height)	Volume
3 units	4 units	2 units	3 × 4 × 2= 24 cubic units

Number Cube Patterns

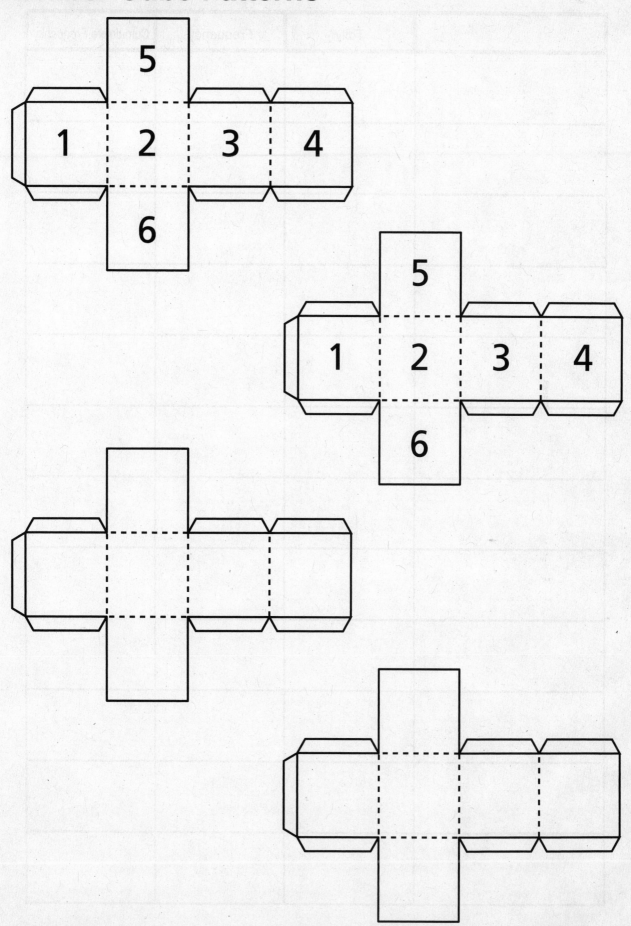

Tally Table

	Tally	Frequency	Cumulative Frequency

Protractor Pattern

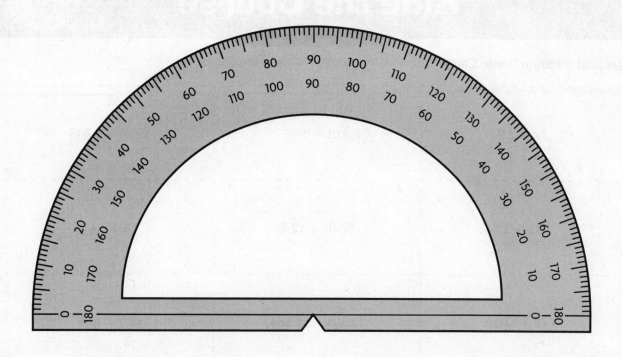

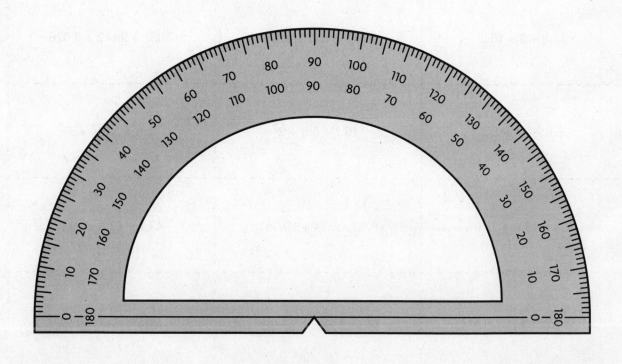

Ride the Course

Game
CARD

Decimal Addition Game Cards

3.4 + 2.9	5.01 + 0.06	2.601 + 4.703
18.9 + 3.1	56.02 + 12.7	8 + 2.4
0.45 + 1.026	12.105 + 15.864	47.2 + 1.95
31.28 + 45.97	2.43 + 5.96	9.005 + 6.15
12.3 + 9 + 10.2	26.01 + 10.7 + 9.233	7.051 + 9.142 + 3.026
6.95 + 4 + 1.2	16.1 + 3.9 + 2	2.6 + 3.8 + 4.5
2.5 + 12.6 + 11.9	8.63 + 0.14 + 19.351	43.1 + 67.8 + 19.7
0.001 + 9.237 + 6.417	13.12 + 10.76 + 12.09	1.05 + 0.15 + 5.01

Ride the Course

Decimal Subtraction Game Cards

15.3 – 12.1	26.5 – 16.7	9 – 1.85
72.3 – 8.6	14.891 – 8.03	0.25 – 0.159
1.3 – 0.536	28.23 – 14.17	6.75 – 5.91
38.001 – 7.25	5.1 – 0.003	33.762 – 1.005
0.865 – 0.13	5.42 – 3.168	48.6 – 18.09
0.875 – 0.625	5.9 – 4.3	18.5 – 4.16
29.54 – 28.59	0.013 – 0.003	76.017 – 35.91
19.005 – 12.16	32.9 – 26.05	8.7 – 4.311

Coordinate Planes

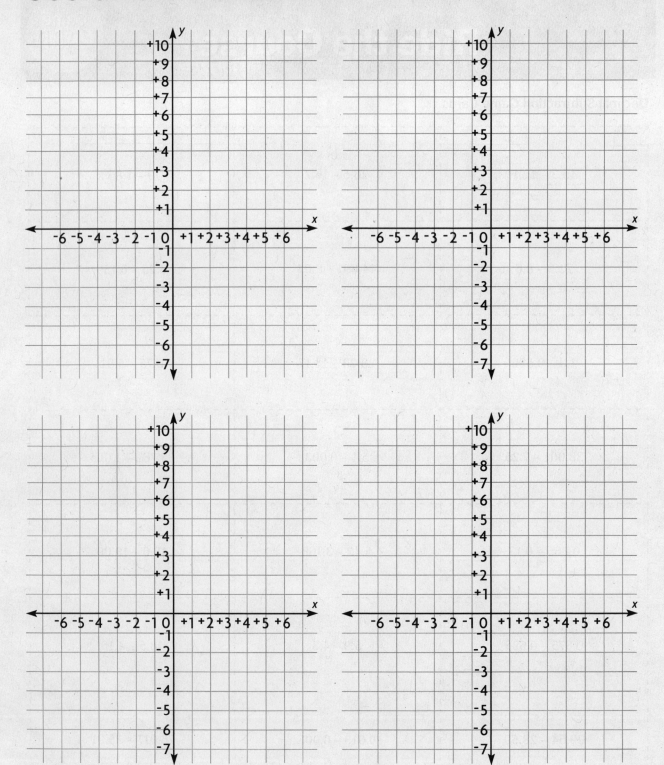

Match Up

Division Cards

37.4 ÷ 6	11.5 ÷ 3	40.9 ÷ 6
66.4 ÷ 8	160.4 ÷ 32	143.2 ÷ 71
265.8 ÷ 87	800.3 ÷ 92	2.5 ÷ 3
1.1 ÷ 6	3.4 ÷ 7	5.9 ÷ 8

Estimate Cards

6	4	7
8	5	2
3	9	0.8
0.2	0.5	0.7

Compatible Number Cards

36 ÷ 6	12 ÷ 3	42 ÷ 6
64 ÷ 8	150 ÷ 30	140 ÷ 70
270 ÷ 90	810 ÷ 90	2.4 ÷ 3
1.2 ÷ 6	3.5 ÷ 7	5.6 ÷ 8

Workmat 1
Place-Value Chart

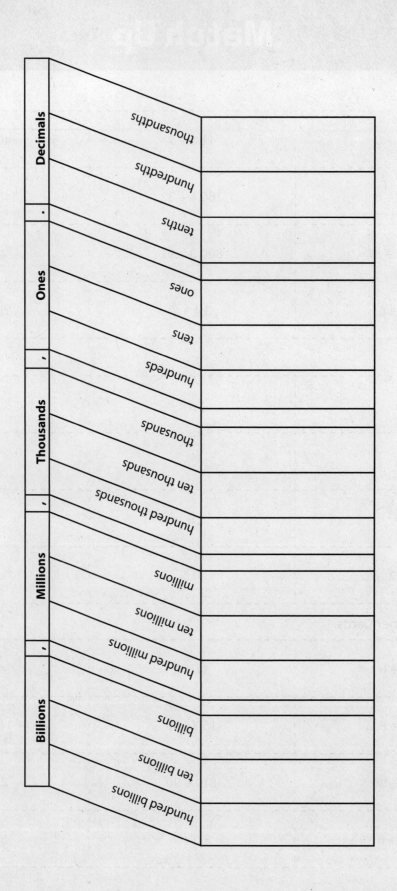

Billions			Millions			Thousands			Ones			.	Decimals	
hundred billions	ten billions	billions	hundred millions	ten millions	millions	hundred thousands	ten thousands	thousands	hundreds	tens	ones	tenths	hundredths	thousandths

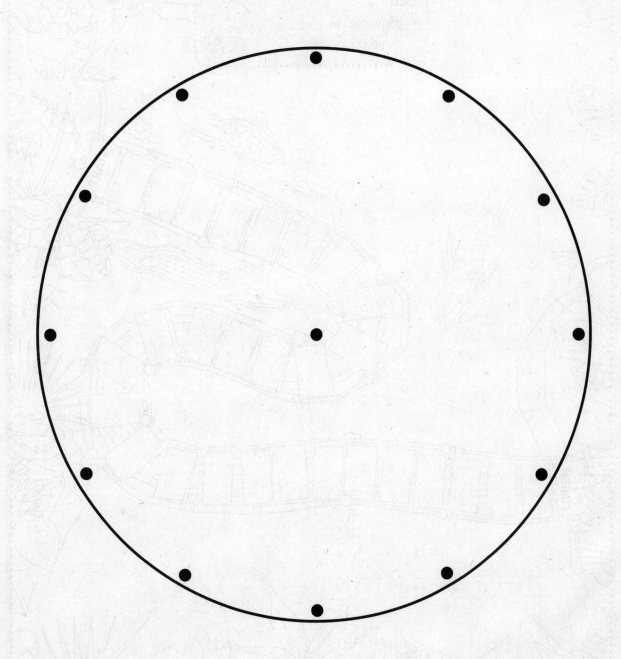

2 Steps Forward, 1 Step Back

Ready!
2 students
Set!
■ game pieces
■ game cards

START

FINISH

A yard and a meter are about the same size.	6 ft = 72 in.
Three feet of rope is the same as 30 inches of rope.	One and one-half yards of fabric is the same as 54 inches of fabric.
One and one-fourth hours before 6:15 is 5 o'clock.	Three and one-half hours after 2:45 is 6:15.
The change in temperature from 34°F to 50°F is 17°F.	The change in temperature from 63°C to 42°C is 21°C.
A metric ton is about 200 pounds.	A ton of gold is 2,000 pounds.
2 L = 2,000 mL	2 gal = 6 qt
A football weighs about 14 pounds.	A truck weighs about 4,000 kg.
40 oz = $2\frac{1}{2}$ lb	500 g = 5 kg
2 cm = 2 m	2 cm = 20 mm
500 m = 50 cm	7 m = 700 cm
4 km = 400,000 mm	6 km = 6,000 m
10 g = 1,000 mg	12 qt = 24 pt
20 in. = 2 ft	5 yd = 15 ft